MIGUEL BARCLAY

STUDENT ONE POUND MEALS

First published in 2022 by HEADLINE HOME
An imprint of HEADLINE PUBLISHING GROUP

1

Cataloguing in Publication Data is available from the British Library

Trade paperback ISBN 9781035401192
eISBN 9781035401185

The recipes in this volume were previously published in the following titles:
One Pound Meals, 9781472245618. 2017
Fast & Fresh One Pound Meals, 9781472245632, 2017
Super Easy One Pound Meals, 9781472254399, 2018
Vegan One Pound Meals, 9781472263728, 2019
Meat-Free One Pound Meals, 9781472264077, 2019
Storecupboard One Pound Meals, 9781472273420, 2020
Green One Pound Meals, 9781472273406, 2021

Designed and typeset by EM&EN
Printed and bound in Great Britain by Clays Ltd, Elcograf S.p.A.

Headline's policy is to use papers that are natural, renewable and recyclable
products and made from wood grown in sustainable forests. The logging and
manufacturing processes are expected to conform to the environmental
regulations of the country of origin.

MIX
Paper from
responsible sources
FSC® C104740

HEADLINE PUBLISHING GROUP
An Hachette UK Company
Carmelite House
50 Victoria EmbankmentLondon
EC4Y 0DZ

www.headline.co.uk
www.hachette.co.uk

CONTENTS

INTRODUCTION

The One Pound Meals series was born out of my obsession with creating simpler and more straightforward recipes. I had been experimenting with this style of cooking for a decade before my first book, it just didn't have a catchy name, until one afternoon I challenged myself to make a paella for £1, posted the dish on Instagram and the rest is history.

Over the years, I must have spent hundreds of hours in the kitchen tinkering with recipes. This is my passion. However, I am more of an anti-chef than a chef – instead of adding ingredients to make a dish stand out, I actually take ingredients away and find shortcuts. And this was how the One Pound Meals series started, from my experimental style of cooking, trying to find the shortest way to tastier food on a budget.

After the success of my paella, I started working to a £1 budget, and found that my unique approach to cooking became a bigger part of the dishes I was creating. As I stripped back dishes even further, recipes became even easier. My recipes got healthier, too – pre-prepared and processed foods were way too expensive, so everything had to be made from scratch using fresh ingredients.

Each recipe in this book has been created using ingredients that add up to £1 or less – with the exception of salt, pepper and oil, which almost everyone has to hand. For the purposes of these recipes, only the amount of ingredients actually used in the recipe have been costed. However, most ingredients are sold in packs that are much larger than you'll need for one portion. But, by focusing on important core ingredients, you won't be left with something you'll only use once. Instead, you'll be able to use the remaining ingredients in different recipes, and that way you can navigate your way around the book depending on what you have in your fridge.

Most of the recipes serve one person. If you've got company, just multiply the ingredients.

This is a relaxed style of cooking, so measurements are purposefully vague. 'A handful' of this or 'a pinch' of that may vary wildly from person to person, but the truth is that it just doesn't matter. If quantities and methods are mega important then they are specified, but otherwise feel free to chuck in whatever quantities you have left in the fridge. This is an approachable style of cooking that fits around your existing routine, using familiar ingredients that you are probably already comfortable with handling and preparing.

MIGUEL BARCLAY

HANGOVER BREAKFASTS

ULTIMATE £1 HANGOVER CURE

One of the great unanswered questions of modern times is: how do you double the amount of cheese in a grilled cheese sandwich without it just spilling out of the sides? The answer is simple. Bind it together with macaroni and be as reckless as you dare.

To make one portion

- 2 slices of bread
- Butter, for spreading
- Small handful of macaroni
- Handful of grated mature Cheddar cheese
- Splash of Worcestershire sauce
- Tabasco sauce
- Sprinkle of celery salt
- Glass of tomato juice
- Salt and pepper

To cook

Lightly butter both sides of the bread slices and gently pan-fry them until golden brown on both sides. Meanwhile, bring a pan of salted water to the boil and cook the macaroni until al dente, then drain and return it to the empty saucepan. Add the grated cheese and gently stir, over a very low heat, until the cheese is fully melted.

Pile the macaroni cheese filling between the pieces of toasted bread and create the tallest cheese sandwich you possibly can.

For the Virgin Bloody Mary, add the Worcestershire sauce, some Tabasco sauce, celery salt and loads of pepper to the glass of tomato juice.

Forget all about last night as you tuck into your ultimate £1 hangover cure, then sit yourself in front of the telly with your duvet.

YOGURT & HONEY POT

When I first moved to London, I used to get these on the way to work every day and eat them at my desk. But this was an expensive habit, so one day I had a go at making them myself and never looked back.

To make one portion

Handful of rolled oats

Handful of trail mix (just nuts and dried fruit)

3 tbsp honey

½ mug of Greek yogurt

To cook

Preheat your oven to 190°C/gas mark 5. Combine the oats, trail mix and 1 tablespoon of the honey in a bowl then spread the mixture out evenly on a baking tray. Bake in the oven for 10 minutes until lightly toasted. Remove from the oven and leave to cool. In a jar, add the rest of the honey, then the yogurt and top with your homemade crunchy granola.

HAM & CHEESE CRÊPES

There's a guy near me who sells these for £5 each, and on Sundays the queue is a mile long! So, I just couldn't resist the challenge, and I created my own super-easy and delicious version for a tenth of the price. As with a lot of my One Pound Meals, you can use these recipes as templates and add whatever ingredients you may have in the fridge. My favourite filling is ham and cheese, but why not try goats' cheese and spinach? Or, go for the insanely popular chocolate-spread filling? Give yourself a treat every Sunday with these One Pound Meals crêpes.

To make one portion (2 crêpes)

50g plain flour

1 egg

150ml milk

Handful of grated cheese

1 slice of ham

Olive oil

Salt and pepper

To cook

In a bowl or jug, whisk together the flour, egg and milk with a pinch of salt.

Preheat a large frying pan over a medium-high heat. Very lightly grease it with oil, then pour half the crêpe mixture into the pan, tilting it to ensure the batter spreads evenly to the edges of the pan.

After about 1 minute, check the underside is cooked and starting to turn golden brown, then carefully flip the crêpe to cook the other side.

While the other side is cooking, add half the cheese and ham to one half of the crêpe and, as the cheese starts to melt, fold the crêpe in half. Cook for a little longer then fold in half again, and then once more. Repeat with the rest of the crêpe mixture and filling to make a second crêpe.

PESTO BRUNCH EGGS

Adding the pesto before you fry your eggs means it incorporates into the eggs as they set, giving you delicious pesto-infused eggs: perfect served for brunch with some potatoes and spinach.

To make one portion

- 1 potato, chopped into 2cm dice (no need to peel)
- 1 tbsp shop-bought pesto
- 2 eggs
- A few cherry tomatoes, quartered
- Handful of spinach
- Handful of grated Parmesan cheese
- Olive oil
- Salt and pepper

To cook

Preheat your oven to 180°C/gas mark 4. Spread out the diced potato on a baking tray. Drizzle with olive oil and season with a pinch of salt. Roast for about 20 minutes, or until cooked through. Remove from the oven and set aside.

Place a frying pan over a medium heat and add the pesto and a glug of olive oil. Break in the eggs and add the tomatoes (keeping the tomatoes on one side of the pan, away from the eggs). Once the eggs are cooked, remove the pan from the heat.

Add the spinach and potatoes to the pan and mix everything together. Once the spinach has wilted, season, then serve topped with a sprinkling of Parmesan cheese.

FRENCH TOAST

One of my favourite brunches ever! Dipping bread into egg is such a simple concept, but the result is amazing. With a few berries and plenty of maple syrup, this makes a special weekend treat.

To make one portion

2 eggs

Pinch of cinnamon

2 slices of white bread

Small knob of butter (or splash of olive oil)

Sprinkle of icing sugar

A generous drizzle of maple syrup

A few blueberries

To cook

Crack the eggs into a dish big enough to lay a slice of bread into. Beat the eggs and add a pinch of cinnamon. Lay the bread in the dish to absorb the egg mixture for about 10 seconds on both sides, then repeat with the second slice.

Heat a frying pan over a medium heat and panfry the bread in some butter or olive oil for a few minutes on each side until the French toast is golden brown.

Transfer to a plate, lightly dust with icing sugar, drizzle with maple syrup and garnish with a few blueberries.

Make it vegan To make this dish vegan, simply pan-fry the bread in vegan butter and cinnamon.

CHORIZO BBQ BEANS

This is one of my favourite brunches ever: smoky BBQ beans with chorizo on sourdough. It's as hearty as a fry-up but takes a fraction of the time and effort. After eating this, you'll realise that normal baked beans just no longer fit the bill.

To make one portion

A few slices of cooking chorizo

¼ red onion, sliced

100g cannellini beans (from a 400g tin), drained

50g passata (from a 400g tin)

Pinch of ground cumin

Pinch of smoked paprika

1 tbsp tomato ketchup

Slice of sourdough bread

Olive oil

Salt and pepper

To cook

Pan-fry the chorizo in a splash of olive oil over a medium heat for a couple of minutes then add the onion and fry for a further couple of minutes until soft. Add the beans, passata, cumin, paprika and ketchup, season with salt and pepper and simmer for about 5 minutes until the sauce is thick and sticky.

Meanwhile, lightly toast the bread. Pour the BBQ beans and chorizo over the bread and sprinkle with some cracked black pepper.

BANANA PANCAKES

This is a great way to use up over-ripe bananas. They create an extra-thick and luxurious pancake batter that will give you gorgeous fluffy pancakes.

To make 4 pancakes

1 ripe banana, peeled

60g self-raising flour

100ml almond milk

1 tbsp caster sugar

Drizzle of golden syrup

To cook

Cut a few slices of the banana and set them aside for a garnish, then mash the rest of the banana in a bowl with the back of a fork, add the self-raising flour, milk and sugar and whisk with a fork to mix.

Pour a quarter of the batter into the centre of a preheated non-stick pan and cook over a medium heat for about 2 minutes, until bubbles start to form on the top and the bottom is golden brown, then flip and cook the other side for about 2 minutes.

Remove from the pan and repeat with the rest of the batter to create 4 pancakes in total. Serve the pancakes in a stack, topped with sliced banana and a drizzle of golden syrup.

SCALLION PANCAKES

With just a handful of ingredients, this is how to make something from nothing. If you want to make the pancakes really flaky, then there is a little bit of extra effort required to create those layers, but it's totally worth it.

To make one portion

75g plain flour

50g water

2 spring onions, sliced, plus extra to serve

1 tsp crispy chilli oil

Salt

Vegetable oil

To cook

Mix together the flour and water in a bowl along with a big pinch of salt. Transfer the mixture to a clean worktop and knead until it comes together to form a dough.

Briefly pan-fry the spring onions in a big glug of olive oil over a medium heat for about 1 minute (and I really do mean a big glug: use about double what you think you should use). Set aside and allow to cool.

Rub some oil on your worktop and squash out the dough to make it as big and flat as you can – aim for a rough rectangle of about 30cm x 10cm. Spread the spring onions and their oil over the dough. Roll the dough lengthways to create a thick sausage, then chop into about 6 sections. Turn each section so the cut sides are on the top and bottom, then squash each one flat with the palm of your hand.

Using the same pan you used for the spring onions, pan-fry the pancakes over a medium heat for a few minutes on each side until golden brown. Serve with some crispy chilli oil and some more sliced spring onion scattered over the top.

PANCAKE STACK

A tall stack of pancakes always looks impressive, so by using this thicker American-style batter recipe, you will be able to recreate exactly the same effect at home. This New York-style brunch manages to bring together both sweet and savoury to create a delicious weekend treat.

To make one portion

75g self-raising flour

15g caster sugar

1 large egg, lightly beaten

60ml milk

10g butter

3 rashers of smoked streaky bacon

Runny honey, for drizzling

To cook

In a jug, whisk together the flour, sugar, egg and milk. Melt the butter (this takes just 10 seconds in the microwave) and pour it into the mixture. Fry the bacon in a pan until crispy. In a separate pre-heated pan, start to cook the pancakes by pouring a small amount of batter into the centre. After about 15 seconds, flip the pancake using a spatula and cook it evenly on both sides. Transfer to a plate and repeat with the rest of the batter.

Stack up the pancakes as high as you can, top with the crispy bacon and drizzle over some honey.

SPANISH OMELETTE

Delicious hot or cold, this is a filling dish that would also make a great packed lunch: you never see people bringing a Spanish omelette to work, but it's perfect for eating on the go. Imagine tucking into one of these for tomorrow's lunch! So, next time you are wondering what to do with the last potato in the bag, don't have a baked potato, try a Spanish omelette. I've even simplified the recipe using a few of my One Pound Meals shortcuts, so there's really no excuse.

To make one portion

1 large potato, diced	4 eggs
20ml water	Olive oil
½ onion, diced	Salt and pepper

To cook

Throw the diced potato in a frying pan, add the water, cover with a lid (or large plate) and steam the potato for about 10 minutes over a medium heat.

Keep an eye on the pan and, once the water has evaporated, remove the lid and throw in the diced onion, a good glug of olive oil and season very generously. Fry over a medium heat until the potato and onion start to colour. At this point, turn the heat down to the lowest setting and crack the eggs into the pan. Mix everything together and cook the omelette very slowly for 10–15 minutes.

Once about 80 per cent of the omelette is cooked, just finish off the top under the grill.

CHEESE SOUFFLÉ OMELETTE

This only takes 5 more minutes than a normal omelette, but the final result will blow your mind. My top tip is to be brave and try to make yours slightly underdone in the middle. Just give it a try!

To make one portion

3 eggs

Handful of finely grated
    Cheddar cheese (if possible
    use a Microplane or very
    fine grater), plus extra for
    garnishing

Olive oil

Pepper

To cook

Preheat the grill to high.

Separate the eggs and whisk the egg whites in a bowl until they form soft peaks. Then in a separate bowl mix the egg yolks with a pinch of pepper and a handful of very finely grated Cheddar.

Gently fold the egg whites and yolks together, then pour into a small oiled preheated frying pan over a medium heat. Cook for exactly 1 minute then cook the top under the grill for another minute.

Fold the omelette in half, garnish with cheese and serve.

CRISPY KALE OVEN OMELETTE

One day I was experimenting with making different flavours of kale crisps and stumbled on an idea for a kale-crisp oven omelette. It's a really simple recipe where all the different textures and flavours come together in the oven to produce an amazing dish.

To make one portion

2 eggs

Handful of kale

Small handful of grated
  Parmesan

Olive oil

Black pepper

To cook

Preheat your oven to 190°C/gas mark 5. Whisk the eggs in a small ovenproof dish. Throw the kale on top and sprinkle with the grated Parmesan and some pepper, then drizzle with olive oil. Cook in the oven for about 15 minutes until the kale is crispy and the eggs are cooked.

THAI OMELETTE

The key to making this dish special is to add a small pinch of curry powder to the beaten egg. This immediately transforms a regular omelette into a fancy Thai-style street food delicacy.

To make one portion

3 eggs, beaten

Pinch of curry powder

Sesame oil

¼ carrot, cut into matchsticks

ó spring onion, cut into strips

A few beansprouts

Drizzle of soy sauce

Salt and pepper

To cook

Season the beaten eggs with salt, pepper and the curry powder. Heat a splash of sesame oil in a frying pan, pour in the beaten eggs and fry for a few minutes until 80% cooked, then add the carrot, spring onion and beansprouts to the middle, drizzle over a little sesame oil and soy sauce, then fold the omelette over the filling and continue to cook for another minute. Remove from the heat and serve with another drizzle of soy sauce to finish.

SHAKSHUKA

This dish has fantastic Middle Eastern flavours that really complement the vibrant and fresh ingredients. It is such a simple dish to make and great to eat as a healthy brunch with a chunk of crusty bread to mop up the sauce.

To make one portion

1 tsp cumin seeds

½ red onion, sliced

¼ yellow pepper, sliced

200g chopped tomatoes (from a 400g tin)

1 egg

Chunk of crusty bread

Olive oil

Salt and pepper

To cook

Toast the cumin seeds in a small dry pan, over a medium heat, until they start to pop, then add a splash of olive oil and the sliced onion. Once the onion starts to soften, add the sliced pepper and chopped tomatoes. Season generously and simmer until the sauce thickens.

Make a small crater in the tomato mixture using the back of a spoon and crack the egg into it, place a lid on the pan and continue to simmer gently until the white is cooked but the yolk is still runny.

Serve in the pan and don't forget to mop up all the juices with some bread.

PIZZA FRITTATA

I love pizza. All the flavours go together perfectly, so I thought I'd try them in a frittata – and it works! For an extra punch, I've used sun-dried tomatoes here instead of fresh ones, and fried the frittata in a splash of the oil that comes with them.

To make one portion

3 eggs

A few sun-dried tomatoes, plus a splash of the oil

A few chunks of torn mozzarella

Pinch of dried oregano

Salt and pepper

To cook

Crack the eggs into a bowl and beat together. Season with salt and pepper, then fry in a pan in a splash of the sun-dried tomato oil over a medium heat for a few minutes until the bottom is cooked.

Preheat the grill to high. Place the sun-dried tomatoes and mozzarella chunks on top of the eggs. Sprinkle over the oregano, then cook under the grill for a few minutes until the eggs are done and the mozzarella has melted.

BREAKFAST ROSTI STACK

This Rosti Stack is a great way to start the morning, with nice vibrant colours on a plate – a satisfying meal to set you up for the day ahead.

To make one portion

Handful of grated or julienned sweet potato

Handful of spinach

½ avocado

Pinch of dried chilli flakes (or dried chillies)

Olive oil

Salt and pepper

To cook

Preheat your oven to 190°C/gas mark 5. Toss the grated or julienned sweet potato in a splash of olive oil, then season with salt and pepper. Assemble a rough pile of the sweet potato in the middle of a baking tray and roast in the oven for about 15 minutes, until the sweet potato is cooked and starting to turn golden brown around the edges.

Meanwhile, wilt the spinach in a hot pan (no oil needed) for a minute or so, and mash the avocado. Season the avocado with salt and pepper.

To assemble the dish, pile the spinach on a plate, put the sweet potato on top, using your hands to shape it into a neat circle, then top with the mashed avocado. Sprinkle with the chilli flakes and serve.

VEGETABLE HASH

A lot of the flavour in this dish comes from the charred and caramelised bits, so don't be scared to leave it in the pan a little longer.

To make one portion

½ courgette	1 egg
½ carrot	Olive oil
½ potato	Salt and pepper

To cook

Grate the courgette, carrot and potato onto a tea towel, sprinkle with salt and wring out as much water as possible by folding the edges of the tea towel together and twisting as hard as you can over the sink. Leave for a few minutes, then repeat to get the last bit of water out.

Heat a frying pan over a medium heat, add a splash of olive oil, then tip the hash into the pan and squash into a thin layer. Season, then leave it to fry gently without touching it for about 5 minutes until the bottom is golden brown. Flip using a fish slice and don't worry if it breaks, it's supposed to look messy. Give it another 5 minutes while you fry an egg in a separate pan and then serve.

CHERRY TOMATO & CHEDDAR SQUARE

This tart, with its base of mature Cheddar cheese and topping of oven-roasted tomatoes, packs a powerful punch. It tastes a bit like pizza but has twice the intensity of flavour. If you are making it for a packed lunch or picnic, then a great idea is to cut the pastry base to exactly the size of your lunchbox, so it fits snugly.

To make one portion

- 15 x 15cm sheet of puff pastry
- A few slices of red onion
- Small handful of grated mature Cheddar cheese
- 8 cherry tomatoes, halved
- Pinch of dried oregano
- Olive oil
- Salt and pepper

To cook

Preheat your oven to 190°C/gas mark 5. Lightly score a 1cm border around the puff pastry sheet with a knife and prick the inside square a few times with a fork (to stop it rising in the oven).

Lay the red onion slices on the puff pastry within the border, then sprinkle over the cheese. Toss the tomatoes in a little olive oil and a pinch of salt and pepper then position them evenly over the tart, cut side up. Finish with a sprinkle of oregano and cook in the oven for about 25 minutes, until the cheese is bubbling and the pastry is golden brown.

STUDY
SNACKS

TOMATOES ON HUMMUS

Adding roasted cherry tomatoes to anything makes it better! They have just the right balance of sweetness and tartness to elevate even the simplest snack to the next level.

To make one portion

Handful of cherry tomatoes

Pinch of dried oregano

2 slices of sourdough bread

2 tbsp hummus

Olive oil

Salt and pepper

To cook

Preheat your oven to 180°C/gas mark 4. Throw the tomatoes into an ovenproof dish. Drizzle with olive oil and sprinkle with salt, pepper and the oregano. Roast in the oven for about 20 minutes until soft and gooey.

Drizzle the sourdough with a little bit of olive oil and scatter over a small pinch of salt, then place in the oven, straight on the wire shelf, for the last 5 minutes of the tomatoes' cooking time. You want the bread to be toasted and nicely brown.

Spread the hummus on the sourdough toast, top with the tomatoes, then drizzle over any juices from the dish you cooked the tomatoes in. Serve straight away.

> **Tip** If you don't think you'll get through a whole loaf of sourdough while it's fresh, slice it up and store it in the freezer so you can just take out one slice at a time to defrost or toast when you need it.

LEMONY PEAS ON TOAST

Avocados are so expensive! So, this is my alternative to the popular vegan brunch option, and it's way more interesting.

To make one portion

Big handful of frozen peas

½ vegetable stock cube

A few slices of ciabatta

A few thin slices of courgette, cut with a potato peeler

Pinch of dried chilli flakes

Wedge of lemon

Olive oil

Salt and pepper

To cook

Put the peas in a pan of salted boiling water, and as soon as the water returns to the boil again, remove from the heat and place half of the peas in a blender along with a couple of tablespoons of the cooking water and the stock cube (draining the remaining peas). Blend to create a purée, season to taste with salt and pepper and stir in the remaining whole peas.

Meanwhile, lightly brush the ciabatta slices with olive oil, season with salt and pepper and either griddle or toast in a dry pan over a high heat for a minute or so on each side until nicely charred.

Spoon the pea purée onto each slice and top with the thinly sliced courgette strips. Sprinkle with the chilli flakes and squeeze over some lemon juice, then serve.

WELSH RAREBIT

Cheese on toast will never be the same again after you've made this. This is next-level cheese on toast and is well worth the extra 30 seconds of effort.

To make one portion

Handful of grated mature
Cheddar cheese

1 egg-cup of single cream

2 slices of bread

2 spring onions, halved

A few splashes of
Worcestershire sauce

Black pepper

To cook

Preheat your grill to high.

Mix the grated cheese and cream together in a bowl to create a cheesy spread with the consistency of mashed potato. Spread it onto the bread slices, top each slice with two halves of spring onion, splash with Worcestershire sauce, then cook under the grill for a few minutes until the cheese melts and starts to brown.

Remove from the grill, sprinkle with cracked black pepper and serve straightaway.

FETA & SUN-DRIED TOMATO FLATBAKES

These wafer-thin tarts have the most amazing crunch and are packed with the intense flavours of sundried tomatoes and baked feta cheese. Cut the folded filo to the exact dimensions of your lunchbox to take your packed lunches to the next level.

To make one portion

- 1 sheet of filo pastry
- Small handful of feta cheese, crumbled
- A few sun-dried tomatoes
- Olive oil
- Black pepper

To cook

Preheat your oven to 190°C/gas mark 5. Fold the filo sheet to make it 3 layers thick, place it on a baking tray, then brush with olive oil and fold in the edges to create an area for the filling. Sprinkle the feta onto the filo and top with sun-dried tomatoes. Bake in the oven for about 15 minutes until the filo is golden brown, then garnish with plenty of cracked black pepper.

PEA & FETA QUESADILLA

My Pea and Feta Quesadilla is a fantastic fresh and light alternative to a traditional quesadilla – jam-packed with vitamins from the peas.

To make one portion

Big handful of frozen peas

40g plain flour, plus extra for dusting

25ml cold water

50g feta cheese, crumbled

Salt and pepper

To cook

Defrost the peas in a colander under the hot tap for 1–2 minutes.

To make the tortilla, mix the flour and water in a bowl with a pinch of salt to form a dough. Dust the worktop with a little flour, then knead the dough on the worktop for a few minutes until smooth. Divide the dough into two balls and roll each piece into a roughly 10cm circle.

Heat a dry frying pan over a high heat, add the tortillas and cook for 20 seconds on each side (just long enough for them to hold their shape).

To make your quesadilla, lightly crush the peas in a bowl with the back of a spoon, then mix them with the crumbled feta and a pinch of salt and pepper. Sandwich the filling between the two tortillas.

Heat a dry frying pan or griddle pan over a high heat. Add the quesadilla and cook for about 5 minutes on each side, until the outside is nicely toasted.

BUTTERNUT QUESADILLA

To create an oozy vegan filling for my quesadilla, I decided to use gooey oven-roasted butternut squash mixed with ground cumin.

To make one portion

¼ butternut squash, peeled and roughly diced

1 tsp ground cumin

1 tsp smoked paprika

2 tbsp tinned black beans

1 spring onion, sliced

40g plain flour, plus extra for dusting

25ml cold water

Olive oil

Salt and pepper

To cook

Preheat your oven to 190°C/gas mark 5. Put the squash in a roasting tray, sprinkle it with the cumin and paprika, drizzle with olive oil and toss to coat, season with salt and pepper and roast in the oven for about 30 minutes until soft. Remove from the oven, mash the butternut squash with a fork, and add the black beans and spring onion.

Meanwhile, mix the flour and water in a bowl with a pinch of salt to form a dough. Dust the worktop with a little flour, then knead the dough for a minute until smooth. Roll into a circle about 20cm in diameter.

Heat a dry frying pan over a high heat, add the tortilla and cook for about 5 seconds to set the shape of the tortilla, then spoon the filling onto one side and fold the tortilla in half. Add a splash of olive oil to the pan and cook the folded quesadilla for about 4 minutes on each side until golden brown. Remove from the heat and serve.

VEGAN SAUSAGE ROLLS

I was really looking forward to creating a Vegan Sausage Roll recipe. It's such an iconic dish that I wanted to take my time and create the best one ever – this is it!

To make one portion

½ red onion, diced

Handful of mushrooms, sliced

2 garlic cloves, sliced

1 tsp dried oregano

200g black beans (from a 400g tin), drained

1 tsp plain flour

½ sheet of ready-rolled puff pastry

Pinch of poppy seeds

Olive oil

Salt and pepper

To cook

Pan-fry the onion in a splash of olive oil over a medium heat for 3 minutes. Add the mushrooms, garlic, oregano and black beans, season with salt and pepper and continue to fry for about 5 minutes until everything is cooked and softened. Remove from the heat, transfer the mixture to a blender and pulse until you get a coarse paste. Tip into a bowl, stir in 1 teaspoon of flour to help the mixture thicken, then allow to cool. Preheat your oven to 190°C/gas mark 5.

Cut the puff pastry into 3 strips approximately 4 x 10cm, spoon in a dollop of filling halfway along the strip and wrap to create your sausage rolls, finishing by squashing the end with the back of a fork. On a lined baking sheet sprinkle each roll with poppy seeds and bake in the oven for about 20 minutes, or until the pastry is golden brown.

CHEESE & ONION POTATO ROLLS

Here's a great veggie alternative to a sausage roll that uses tinned potatoes to make it even easier for you.

To make 4 portions

2 x 300g tins of potatoes, drained

Bunch of spring onions, thinly sliced

Big handful of grated Cheddar cheese

1 sheet of frozen puff pastry, defrosted

1 egg, beaten

Salt and pepper

To cook

Preheat your oven to 180°C/gas mark 4 and line a baking tray with greaseproof paper. Grab a bowl, tip in the potatoes and mash them with a fork. Season, then mix in the spring onions and Cheddar.

Cut the puff pastry into four rectangles 15 x 17cm. Add a tablespoon of the filling to each rectangle and roll up from the short end. Lay the rolls on the lined baking tray, brush with beaten egg and bake for about 25 minutes, or until golden brown.

> **Make ahead** These rolls can be made ahead of time and cooked from frozen.

OOTHAPPAM INDIAN CRUMPETS

These Indian Crumpets are a dairy-free revelation! Rice is the secret ingredient here – it creates gorgeous crumpets with an amazing gooey texture.

To make one portion

1 mug of basmati rice

5 mugs of water

1 mug of self-raising flour

A few broccoli tips

A few slices of red onion

Olive oil

Salt and pepper

To cook

Put the rice and 3 mugs of the water in a saucepan, cover and cook over a medium heat for about 10 minutes, or until all the water has been absorbed and the rice is cooked, then throw it in a blender (while it's hot) along with the self-raising flour, the remaining water and a generous pinch of salt and pepper.

Heat a non-stick frying pan with a glug of olive oil over a medium heat. Dollop 1 tablespoon of the crumpet mixture into the hot pan and fry on one side for about a minute, until it starts to brown (you may need to mix a little more flour into the batter before frying, if it begins to separate). Then, gently push some of the broccoli and onion slices into the uncooked side before flipping it over and cooking it for another minute or so.

Remove from the pan and repeat with more mixture, broccoli and onion. The mixture should make 5 pancakes in total. Serve warm.

SWEETCORN & COURGETTE FRITTERS

If you're ever stuck for vegan snack inspiration, just give these Sweetcorn & Courgette Fritters a go.

To make one portion

½ courgette

Handful of tinned sweetcorn, drained

2 tbsp gram flour (chickpea flour)

Handful of rocket

Olive oil

Salt and pepper

To cook

Grab a bowl and grate the courgette into it, then throw in the sweetcorn and gram flour and season with salt and pepper. Stir everything together until the mixture has a thick batter consistency.

Pan-fry dollops of the mixture in a splash of olive oil over a medium heat, for a couple of minutes on each side, until golden brown (the mixture should make about 4 fritters), then serve with some rocket leaves.

HERB STEM FRITTERS

Ever wondered what to do with all those leftover herb stems? It's easy – stick them into a fritter. Each batch is a total surprise: just use whatever herb stalks you've got.

To make one portion

2 spring onions, sliced

Small handful of frozen peas, defrosted

1 egg, beaten

2 tbsp plain flour

Handful of any leftover cheese (such as Cheddar, Brie or feta), grated, crumbled or finely diced

Handful of leftover herb stalks, finely chopped

Olive oil

Salt and pepper

To cook

In a bowl, mix together the spring onions, peas, egg, flour, cheese and herb stalks. Season with salt and pepper. Place a frying pan over a medium heat and add a splash of olive oil, then use a big serving spoon to add about a quarter of the mixture to the pan in one big dollop. Repeat until you have 4 fritters. Fry them for about 5 minutes on each side, then serve.

CHARRED PEPPERS & BREADCRUMBS

I love to cook with breadcrumbs: they are cheap and versatile, and they elevate a dish by adding texture. Whenever I have leftover bread, I just let it go dry, stick it in the blender to make bread-crumbs (you could also grate it), then store the crumbs in jars.

To make one portion

1½ peppers, in contrasting colours, cut into quarters

½ red onion, finely diced

1 garlic clove, sliced

Handful of breadcrumbs

Small handful of parsley, chopped

Olive oil

Salt and pepper

To cook

Preheat your grill to high.

Cook the peppers under the grill skin-side up until soft and slightly charred.

Meanwhile, pan-fry the onion in a splash of olive oil over a medium heat for a few minutes, then add the garlic and fry for a few more minutes until the garlic starts to brown. Add the breadcrumbs and a splash more olive oil, and season with salt and pepper. Fry for a couple of minutes, until the breadcrumbs are golden brown, then add the chopped parsley and remove from the heat. Serve the peppers topped with the fried breadcrumbs.

SCOTCH EGGS

Ever wondered how Scotch eggs are actually made? Well, it's not as difficult as you'd think, so impress your friends with these fun treats and, if you manage to get a runny yolk, then you know you've nailed it

To make 2 Scotch eggs

3 eggs

1 tbsp plain flour

Big handful of breadcrumbs
(grated stale bread)

200g minced pork

Sunflower oil

Salt and pepper

To cook

Bring a saucepan of water to the boil and cook 2 of the eggs for exactly 7 minutes, then cool them quickly under cold running water to stop the cooking process.

Place the flour and some seasoning in one bowl, beat the third egg in another bowl, and put the breadcrumbs and some seasoning in a third bowl.

Mix the minced pork in a bowl with some salt and pepper.

Peel the 2 cooked and cooled eggs and wrap them with the minced pork. Roll them in the flour, then the beaten egg, then coat in the breadcrumbs.

Turn on the deep-fat fryer to pre-heat, or heat some sunflower oil in a saucepan (about half full). Fry the Scotch eggs for about 10 minutes, until golden brown and the meat is cooked through

LEEK CROQUETTES

These Spanish-style croquettes are made with traditional British leeks and are a great example of how I mix different cooking styles and ingredients in my quest to create tasty economical meals. I hope this inspires you to give them a go.

To make one portion

- 1 large potato, peeled and cut into chunks
- 1 leek, finely diced
- Handful of breadcrumbs
- Olive oil
- Salt and pepper

To cook

Cook the potato chunks in a pan of salted boiling water for about 10 minutes until soft, then drain in a colander and let the water steam off for a few minutes before mashing them.

Meanwhile, season and pan-fry the leek in a splash

of olive oil over a medium heat for about 10 minutes until softened but not browned.

Mix the leek with the mashed potato, season to taste with salt and pepper and allow to cool.

Season the breadcrumbs with salt and pepper.

Once cooled, wet your hands and roll the leek and potato mash into 5 balls, then roll each ball in the seasoned breadcrumbs (the water from your hands will help the breadcrumbs to stick).

Either shallow-fry the croquettes in olive oil, turning them occasionally so they get an even colour, or – for the best results – deep-fry them in hot oil over a medium heat for about 5 minutes, until golden brown. Drain on kitchen paper, then serve.

APPLE & STILTON SLAW

Crispy Stilton croutons piled with a tasty creamy slaw, then topped with slices of apple . . . It's not really a salad but it's definitely more than just a coleslaw.

To make one portion

Small handful of crumbled Stilton

A couple of slices of baguette

½ red onion, sliced

Wedge of red cabbage, sliced

½ carrot, cut into matchsticks

1 tbsp crème fraîche

1 tsp Dijon mustard

A few slices of apple

Salt and pepper

To cook

Preheat your oven to 190°C/gas mark 5. Pile the crumbled Stilton onto the baguette slices and cook on a baking tray for about 10 minutes until the bread is crispy and the cheese has melted.

Meanwhile, to make the slaw, grab a bowl and mix together the onion, cabbage, carrot, crème fraîche and Dijon mustard, then season to taste. Serve with the Stilton croutons and top with a few slices of apple.

BEETROOT CARPACCIO

Get creative with your presentation skills and try this stunning Beetroot Carpaccio. The flavours are fresh and summery, making it ideal for a sophisticated snack.

To make one portion

- 1 pre-cooked beetroot, thinly sliced
- Small handful of crumbled feta cheese
- 1 tsp crème fraîche

- ½ lemon
- Olive oil
- Salt and pepper

To cook

Lay the thinly sliced beetroot on a plate in a circular formation so the edges overlap, then sprinkle over the feta.

To make the dressing, mix the crème fraîche with a big squeeze of lemon juice in a bowl then drizzle it over the beetroot.

Garnish with a few gratings of lemon zest, a splash of olive oil, a tiny pinch of salt and some cracked black pepper.

ON-THE-GO LIBRARY LUNCHES

CAPRESE CLUB

Here I have taken my favourite summer salad, a cool and refreshing Caprese salad, and modified the ingredients to create a club sandwich. Instead of butter, I have used creamy smashed avocado, and also brushed what would be a traditional olive oil dressing lightly on the bread with a pinch of oregano before toasting.

To make one portion

3 slices of bread

Pinch of dried oregano

½ ripe avocado

2 tomatoes, sliced

½ mozzarella ball

Olive oil

Salt and pepper

To cook

Lightly brush the bread slices on both sides with olive oil and scatter with the oregano before toasting on a hot griddle pan or frying pan.

Meanwhile, mash the avocado in a bowl with a pinch of salt and pepper using the back of a fork.

Once toasted, spread the smashed avocado on two of the bread slices, top with the sliced tomatoes and hand-torn chunks of mozzarella. Stack into a club sandwich and top with the final bread slice.

NEW YORK MEATBALL SANDWICH

This recipe takes just 10 minutes to make and is a whole meal in a sandwich. When I was creating the recipe, I used a clever little technique for keeping the bread dry and away from the sauce. Firstly, I pan-toasted the bread to make it crunchier and less absorbent. Then, I took it one step further and melted cheese on one side of each slice, forming a neat little sauce-proof barrier and perfectly finishing off my decadent New York meatball sandwich.

To make one portion

75g minced beef

¼ red onion, finely diced

1 garlic clove, crushed

1 tsp dried oregano

2 slices of bread

Handful of grated Cheddar cheese

200g passata

Olive oil

Salt and pepper

To cook

In a bowl, mix the minced beef with the diced onion, half the crushed garlic and half the oregano, and season with salt and pepper. Form into 4 compact balls and pan-fry over a medium heat with a splash of olive oil until darkly coloured.

Meanwhile, toast the bread slices on both sides in a pan with a splash of olive oil, then sprinkle the grated cheese on one side of each slice and melt under the grill.

When the meatballs are cooked, add the passata to the pan, along with the remaining garlic, oregano and more salt and pepper (keep the meatballs in the pan), and simmer for 1–2 minutes to reduce the sauce slightly.

Make the sandwich with the cheese facing inwards and enjoy your very own taste of New York!

CLUB SANDWICH

Top hotels across the world are judged on this one dish alone. So, let's try and make the best club sandwich in the world for just £1. The bread will make or break your sandwich, so for the most decadent club sandwich, you must always toast your bread in a frying pan or on a griddle using a tiny bit of olive oil, salt and pepper. Without this step, there is no way your bread will hold this many ingredients.

To make one portion

- 2 chicken thighs, skin on and de-boned
- 3 rashers of smoked streaky bacon
- 3 slices of bread
- A few Little Gem lettuce leaves
- 1 tomato, sliced
- Mayo
- Olive oil
- Salt and pepper

To cook

Pan-fry the chicken thighs skin-side down over a medium heat with a splash of olive oil for 7 minutes, then flip and fry for a further 7 minutes, until golden brown and cooked through. Remove from the pan to rest while you fry the bacon.

Meanwhile, for the bread, lightly drizzle some olive oil on each side, season with salt and pepper, and fry over a medium heat in a frying pan or on a griddle until golden brown.

Arrange your sandwich by placing one slice of bread on a board, adding a layer of lettuce, then tomato, a tiny bit of cracked black pepper, the chicken thighs and a generous dollop of mayo. Then, add the middle slice of bread and repeat the layers, this time adding the bacon. Then finish the dish with the third slice of bread, securing it with a wooden skewer to stop it toppling over.

SWEET POTATO FALAFEL WRAP

Making falafel at home can seem a little daunting, so here's the easiest recipe you'll ever find!

To make one portion

- 1 sweet potato
- 1 tsp ground cumin
- 2 spring onions, chopped
- 1 tbsp sesame seeds
- 40g plain flour
- 25ml cold water
- Handful of sliced red cabbage
- A few tomatoes, chopped
- Handful of sliced white onion
- Olive oil
- Salt and pepper

To cook

Preheat your oven to 190°C/gas mark 5. Pierce the sweet potato several times with a fork and bake it in the oven for 30 minutes, or cook it in the microwave for 10 minutes, until soft. Once it's cool enough to handle, cut it in half, scoop the flesh into a bowl, season it with salt and pepper and mix in the cumin and half the spring onion.

Wet your hands to stop the mixture sticking to them, then roll it into balls about the same size as a ping-pong ball. Roll the balls in the sesame seeds, place them on a baking tray, drizzle with olive oil and bake in the oven for 30 minutes.

Meanwhile, make the flatbread wrap. Mix the flour and water in a bowl with a pinch of salt to form a dough. Knead on the worktop for a few minutes until smooth, then roll it out into a 20cm diameter circle. Cook in a dry preheated pan over a high heat for about 2 minutes on each side until nicely toasted.

Assemble the wrap by topping the flatbread with the falafel and adding the red cabbage, chopped tomatoes, sliced onion and remaining spring onion.

CURRIED SQUASH TURNOVER

A beautiful, soft and gooey curried squash filling, surrounded by a crispy, flaky pastry crust.

To make one portion (2 turnovers)

A few cubes of peeled and chopped butternut squash

½ onion, sliced

1 tsp curry powder

2 squares of puff pastry, approximately 10 × 10cm

1 egg, beaten (optional)

Olive oil

Salt and pepper

To cook

Preheat your oven to 180°C/gas mark 4.

Place the squash cubes on a baking tray. Drizzle with olive oil, then sprinkle with salt, black pepper and the curry powder. Roast for about 30 minutes, adding the onions halfway through. Remove from the oven (leave the oven on) and allow to cool a little, then crush very slightly with a fork.

Line a clean baking tray with greaseproof paper and place the pastry squares on the lined tray. Spoon half of the filling into the middle of each square, then fold in half diagonally and gently seal the edges of the pastry by applying light pressure with your fingertips or the back of a fork.

Brush with egg, if you wish, then bake for about 20 minutes or until golden brown. Enjoy straight away or allow to cool and take them with you as a packed lunch – these are just as delicious cold.

> **Swap** If you don't want to use an egg wash, brush the turnovers with a little oat milk before baking.

SUN-DRIED TOMATO PASTA

This pasta sauce requires no cooking, so it's the sort of recipe that will help you reclaim your free time while still eating delicious food made from scratch.

To make one portion

½ jar sun-dried tomatoes in oil, plus the oil

A few sprigs of basil

Handful of grated Parmesan cheese

125g pasta of your choice

Olive oil

Salt and pepper

To cook

Cook the pasta in a pan of salted boiling water according to the packet instructions. Once cooked, drain and save a little of the pasta water.

Meanwhile, put the sun-dried tomatoes in a blender, along with the oil from the jar, the basil and the Parmesan. Blitz to form a smooth paste and season to taste.

Stir the paste into the cooked pasta, adding a splash of the pasta water to loosen. Serve immediately.

> **Tip** Feel free to mix and match your pasta shapes to use everything up.

GREEK SALAD ORZO

Here I have made my ultimate packed-lunch salad, using orzo pasta and tangy feta cheese.

To make 4 portions

150g orzo pasta

½ cucumber, chopped

Handful of cherry tomatoes, quartered

Handful of black olives, sliced

1 red onion, thinly sliced

100g feta cheese, cubed

A few pinches of dried oregano

½ lemon

Olive oil

Salt and pepper

To cook

Boil the orzo in salted water according to the packet instructions, then drain, drizzle with a little olive oil and allow to cool.

Once cooled, mix with the cucumber, tomatoes, olives, onion, feta and a pinch of oregano, then season with salt and pepper. Dress with a squeeze of lemon juice and a drizzle of olive oil. Finish with a final pinch of oregano.

> **Make it vegan** To make this dish vegan, swap the feta for a plant-based cheese.

LETTUCE BURRITO BUDDHA BOWL

This lighter and fresher version of a burrito uses a lettuce leaf as a bowl.

To make one portion

- ½ mug of basmati rice
- 1 mug of water
- Handful of tinned red kidney beans, drained
- 1 tsp ground cumin
- A few tomatoes, roughly chopped
- ¼ red onion, roughly chopped
- Small handful of tinned sweetcorn, drained
- 1 round lettuce leaf
- Olive oil
- Salt and pepper

To cook

Put the rice and water in a saucepan and cook over a medium heat with the lid on for about 7 minutes. When all the water has been absorbed and the rice is cooked, turn off the heat, remove the lid and fluff up the rice with a fork.

While the rice is cooking, pan-fry the kidney beans with the cumin in a splash of olive oil over a medium heat for a few minutes until they start to pop. Season with salt and pepper and set to one side.

To make the salsa, mix the tomatoes with the red onion in a bowl, season with salt and pepper and dress with a drizzle of olive oil.

Assemble the Buddha Bowl inside the lettuce leaf by adding the rice, then adding the sweetcorn, salsa and kidney beans.

BROCCOLI & NOODLE SALAD WITH PEANUT DRESSING

I serve this dish at room temperature, but it is equally delicious served cold as a packed lunch. Just make sure you don't overcook the broccoli stems – you want to keep some crunch.

To make one portion

- 1 nest of wholewheat noodles (check the packet if you're vegan)
- A few pieces of long-stem broccoli
- 1 garlic clove, grated
- 4 tbsp soy sauce
- juice of ½ lime
- 2 tbsp sesame oil
- 1 tbsp peanut butter (crunchy or smooth)
- Sprinkle of sesame seeds, to garnish

To cook

Cook the noodles in a pan of boiling water according to the packet instructions. Cook the broccoli in the same pan at the same time until cooked but still firm – it will take about 5 minutes. Drain the broccoli and noodles and allow to cool a bit.

Meanwhile, make the sauce. In a bowl, mix together the garlic, soy sauce, lime juice, sesame oil and peanut butter. If the sauce is too thick, add a little water to thin it out.

Drizzle the sauce over the broccoli and noodles, then garnish with a sprinkle of sesame seeds.

OVEN-ROASTED MOROCCAN VEG & COUSCOUS

Couscous is such a versatile ingredient: it can take on strong flavours and pad out veg to create a main meal. This is a great recipe for preparing in advance.

To make one portion

½ red onion, diced

½ red pepper, diced

½ courgette, diced

½ carrot, diced

¼ mug of couscous

½ tsp of cumin

Small handful of raisins

½ mug of boiling water

Small handful of flaked almonds

Small handful of chopped parsley

Olive oil

Salt and pepper

To cook

Spread out the diced onion, pepper, courgette and carrot on a baking tray. Drizzle with olive oil and sprinkle over a pinch of salt and pepper, then roast for 15–20 minutes.

Meanwhile, put the couscous, cumin and raisins in a bowl. Pour over the boiling water and leave for 10 minutes so the couscous can absorb the water. Fluff with a fork, then mix in the roasted veg. Season to taste, add a splash of olive oil, and serve garnished with flaked almonds and chopped parsley.

AMERICAN CHOPPED SALAD

This is how Americans do salad. I thought it was a bit strange at first, but it actually does taste better – I'm not sure if it's psychological or if the flavours just mix better this way!

To make one portion

- 1 tbsp mayonnaise
- 1 tsp Dijon mustard
- 1 chicken thigh, deboned, skin removed
- 1 slice of bread, chopped into 1cm cubes
- A few lettuce leaves, chopped into 1cm pieces

- ½ avocado, chopped into 1cm cubes
- 1 tomato, chopped into 1cm cubes
- 2 tbsp tinned sweetcorn
- Olive oil
- Salt and pepper

To cook

First, make the dressing by mixing the mayo and mustard with 3 tablespoons olive oil in a small bowl. Set aside.

Season the chicken with salt and pepper, then pan-fry in a splash of oil over a medium heat for about 7 minutes on each side until cooked through. Remove chicken from the pan (leaving the juices) and chop it into 1cm cubes.

Add the bread cubes to the same pan and fry over a medium heat for a few minutes until nicely golden and toasted.

Add the chopped lettuce, avocado and tomato to a bowl, along with the chicken, croutons and sweetcorn. Season to taste and drizzle with the dressing.

> **Swap** To make it veggie, why not swap the chicken for some leftover roasted sweet potatoes or squash?

PEA, MINT & FETA SALAD

This recipe is just so easy, and it's more of an interesting and substantial dish than a traditional salad made with lettuce and tomato.

To make one portion

Big handful of frozen peas

Small handful of frozen broad beans

Handful of chopped mint

1 red chilli, sliced

Small handful of crumbled feta

Olive oil

Salt and pepper

To cook

Put the peas and broad beans in a colander and run hot water from the tap over them until they have defrosted, then shell the broad beans. Tip into a bowl, dress with a splash of olive oil and season with a pinch each of salt and pepper, then add the mint, chilli and feta and mix to combine.

MEXICAN KIDNEY BEAN SALAD

I use kidney beans all the time to bulk out meals, but they need a bit of care and attention to get the best out of them. My favourite technique is to pan-fry them in cumin, which makes the skins split and allows the flavour to penetrate.

To make one portion

Handful of tinned red kidney beans, drained

1 tsp ground cumin

1 spring onion, roughly chopped

1 egg-cup of couscous

1 egg-cup of water

Small handful of tinned sweetcorn, drained

A few cherry tomatoes, quartered

Small handful of rocket

Olive oil

Salt and pepper

To cook

Pan-fry the kidney beans in a splash of olive oil over a medium heat with the cumin for a few minutes until the skins start to split. Season with salt and pepper, add the spring onion and cook for a few more minutes until softened. Remove from the heat and add the couscous, stirring to coat it in the cumin-infused oil. Add the water, stir, and leave for a few minutes for the couscous to plump up.

Season the couscous to taste then combine with the sweetcorn, cherry tomatoes and rocket in a bowl. Mix together and dress with a glug of olive oil, then serve.

SMASHED CUCUMBER SALAD

All too often, cucumber can be a bit boring, so you know a recipe that uses cucumber as the main ingredient has to be exceptional. The fresh, spicy flavours here make the simple ingredients more exciting.

To make one portion

½ cucumber

A few cherry tomatoes, halved

1 garlic clove, crushed or grated

1 red chilli, sliced

1 tsp crispy chilli oil

1 tsp rice wine vinegar

1 tsp sesame oil

1 tsp soy sauce

Salt

To make

Lightly bash the cucumber with a heavy object like a rolling pin (this will increase its surface area and make it easier to get the excess liquid out), then slice the cucumber in half lengthways. Scrape out the seeds (see Tip), then slice the cucumber into 1cm thick slices, cutting at an angle. Place them in a bowl with a pinch of salt and leave to rest for 10 minutes, then discard any the liquid that comes out of the cucumber. Now add the tomatoes, garlic, chilli, crispy chilli oil, rice wine vinegar, sesame oil and soy sauce to the bowl. Mix to combine, then serve.

> **Tip** Try stirring the cucumber seeds into some yogurt with a little mint to make a tzatziki.

CARROT & CORIANDER SALAD

The trick to this salad is to use fresh coriander, and marinate everything in lime juice: squeezing fresh lime over the salad and leaving it for 10 minutes means the raw onion 'cooks' lightly in the acidity and softens up to create a nice mellow flavour.

To make one portion

Handful of thinly sliced red cabbage

¼ red onion, thinly sliced

Handful of chopped coriander

¼ carrot, cut into thin matchsticks

½ lime

Olive oil

Salt and pepper

To make

Mix the cabbage and onion in a bowl with the coriander and carrot. Squeeze over the lime juice, add a splash of olive oil and a pinch each of salt and pepper, then leave it to rest for at least 10 minutes before serving.

TOFU SALAD

This Vietnamese-inspired recipe contrasts the summery flavours of mint with spicy chilli and sharp lime to create a perfectly balanced dish.

To make one portion

2 tbsp sesame oil

2 tbsp soy sauce

2 tbsp golden syrup

Pinch of grated ginger

Pinch of dried chilli flakes

1 garlic clove, crushed

¼ lime

100g firm tofu, cubed

½ sheet of dried vermicelli noodles

½ gem lettuce, roughly chopped

¼ carrot, cut into matchsticks

Small handful of peanuts

A few fresh mint leaves

To make

Mix the sesame oil, soy sauce, golden syrup, grated ginger, chilli flakes, crushed garlic and the juice of the lime in a bowl. Add the tofu, stir to coat and leave it to marinate for 10 minutes while you prepare the rest of the salad.

Meanwhile, blanch the noodles briefly in boiling water, according to the packet instructions. Drain.

Mix together the drained noodles in a bowl with the chopped lettuce, carrot, peanuts and mint leaves. Add the tofu, pour over the remaining marinade, then serve.

LAZY
WEEKEND
LUNCHES

STUFFED ROLLS

This is an unconventional and fun way to make a sandwich. Don't just cut open a bread roll lengthways and have one layer of flavour – go crazy and really increase that filling-to-bread ratio.

To make one portion

- 1 bread roll (any kind you like)
- A few slices of mozzarella (or any bits of cheese you have in the fridge)
- A few slices of roasted peppers from a jar
- 2 tbsp pesto
- Fresh basil leaves, to serve (optional)

To cook

Preheat the oven to 180°C/gas mark 4. Cut a series of slits in your bread, working your way down the length, but don't cut all the way through. Spread some pesto into each slit, then stuff with the peppers and mozzarella slices. Bake for about 5 minutes or until the cheese has melted, then serve with another dollop of pesto on top, plus a few basil leaves (if using).

GRILLED CAULIFLOWER CHEESE SANDWICH

Here's a twist on a grilled cheese sandwich: adding cauliflower. It makes for a decadent and filling sandwich. Don't forget to use the cauliflower leaves – I promise they are delicious and should never be thrown away.

To make one portion

A few cauliflower florets, broken into small pieces, plus some leaves

1 tsp butter

1 tsp plain flour

100ml milk

Small handful of Cheddar cheese

2 slices of bread

Olive oil

Salt and pepper

To cook

Season the cauliflower florets and pan-fry in a splash of olive oil over a medium heat for about 5 minutes. After about 3 minutes, add the leaves (removing any tough bits of stalk), followed by the butter. Once the butter has melted, add the flour, then continue to cook for a further minute. Slowly add the milk, a little at a time, stirring constantly. Once you have a creamy sauce, remove from the heat and stir in the cheese.

Meanwhile, drizzle the bread with olive oil and season with a sprinkle of salt, then either toast in a griddle or frying pan over a medium heat, or place under the grill. Pile the cauliflower cheese on to one of the slices of toasted bread, then top with the other slice and serve as a sandwich.

> **Tip** Try swapping the cauliflower for broccoli – and switch up the Cheddar for whatever cheese you have in the fridge.

CHEESE & TOMATO PUFF PASTRY QUICHE

Imagine how many more quiches you'd make if it wasn't such a time-consuming process. Well, now there's no excuse. Here, the pastry is pre-made and you don't need to sweat down any onions: just throw the raw ingredients together and bake.

To make one portion

- 1 square of puff pastry
- 3 eggs, beaten
- Handful of grated Cheddar cheese
- A few cherry tomatoes, halved
- Olive oil
- Salt and pepper

To cook

Preheat your oven to 190°C/gas mark 5.

Grease an ovenproof dish or pan with oil, cut the puff pastry to roughly fit (don't worry about trimming the edges), then line the dish or pan with it.

Combine the beaten eggs and grated cheese and season with salt and pepper. Pour the mixture into the dish or pan, then top with the tomato halves, cut-side up. To get a lovely golden crust, brush some of the egg filling onto the edges of the pastry, then bake in the oven for about 30 minutes until the pastry is golden brown and the filling is set.

Remove the quiche from the oven, sprinkle with salt and pepper, and serve hot or cold.

SLOPPY JOES

My favourite thing about a Sloppy Joe is the slow-cooked caramelised red onions, so I created this dish, which is overloaded with caramelised red onions then oven-baked, to intensify the flavour even more.

To make one portion

2 red onions, sliced

2 garlic cloves, crushed

200g chopped tomatoes (from a 400g tin)

1 part-baked baguette, cut into 2.5cm-thick slices

Pinch of dried parsley

Olive oil

Salt and pepper

To cook

Slowly pan-fry the onions in a splash of olive oil over a low-medium heat, with a pinch each of salt and pepper, for about 20 minutes, until sweet and sticky. Add half the crushed garlic and fry for another few minutes then add the chopped tomatoes and simmer for about 15 minutes until the onion and tomato mixture has a thick consistency. Season to taste with salt and pepper.

Meanwhile, preheat your oven to 190°C/gas mark 5.

Grab a small ovenproof dish or tray, add a glug of olive oil, then add half the slices of bread. Spoon the onion and tomato filling over each slice and top with the remaining slices of bread.

Mix together the remaining crushed garlic with a glug of olive oil and the parsley. Brush the top layer with the mixture then bake in the oven for 25 minutes, until the bread is golden brown. Remove from the oven and serve.

POLENTA CHIP KEBAB

This is my vegan version of the classic Friday night Chip Kebab.

To make one portion

2 mugs of water for the polenta, plus 50ml cold water for the pita

Pinch of dried oregano

½ mug of polenta

80g self-raising flour

Small handful of sliced red cabbage

Small handful of sliced lettuce

Small handful of chopped tomatoes

Olive oil

Salt and pepper

To cook

Bring the 2 mugs of water to the boil in a saucepan, adding a pinch of salt, pepper and the oregano. Turn the heat down to medium, then slowly add the polenta while stirring with a whisk. Stir continuously for about 10 minutes until thick, then pour into a square high-sided tray or dish and leave to cool for an hour or so in the fridge. Preheat your oven to 190°C/gas mark 5 and line a baking tray with greaseproof paper.

Once the polenta has cooled and formed a solid block, remove it from the tray and slice it into chip-shaped rectangles. Place them on the lined baking tray, drizzle with olive oil, toss to coat and cook in the oven for 25 minutes until golden brown and crunchy on the outside.

Meanwhile, mix together the flour and water in a bowl along with a pinch of salt to form a dough. Knead for 1 minute on the work-top until smooth, then shape into a rough oval about 10cm long.

Preheat a dry frying pan over a high heat and cook the pita bread in the hot pan for about 2 minutes on each side until puffed up and nicely toasted. To serve, cut open the pita bread, fill with the cabbage, lettuce and tomatoes and the polenta chips.

ROAST CHICKPEA GYROS

Oven-roasting chickpeas with olive oil, cumin and paprika creates an intensely flavoured filling for a gyro. The chickpeas have a slight crunch and are perfect for wrapping in a warm flatbread with loads of salad and a creamy sauce.

To make one portion

- 200g chickpeas (from a 400g tin), drained
- 1 tsp ground cumin
- 1 tsp smoked paprika
- 40g plain flour, plus extra for dusting
- 25ml cold water
- 2 tbsp crème fraîche
- Pinch of dried oregano
- A few lettuce leaves
- A few cherry tomatoes, chopped
- A few slices of red onion
- Olive oil
- Salt and pepper

To cook

Preheat your oven to 190°C/gas mark 5.

Put the chickpeas in an ovenproof dish with a glug of olive oil, the cumin, paprika and a pinch each of salt and pepper. Roast in the oven for about 20 minutes until golden brown.

Meanwhile, to make the flatbread, mix the flour and water in a bowl with a pinch of salt to form a dough. Dust the worktop with a little flour, then knead the dough for a minute until smooth. Roll into a circle about 20cm in diameter.

Heat a dry frying pan or griddle over a high heat, add the flatbread and cook for a minute on each side until nicely toasted.

Make the sauce by mixing the crème fraîche in a bowl with a pinch each of salt and pepper and the oregano, then assemble the gyro by stuffing the flatbread with lettuce, tomato, onion, sauce and roasted chickpeas, then folding it in half.

POTATO & LEEK SLICE

This is my version of the famous Greggs cheese and onion slice and is packed with so much flavour. Best eaten in slices.

To make one portion

1 potato, diced

1 leek, sliced

Small handful of grated
   Cheddar cheese

20 x 20cm sheet of puff pastry

1 egg, beaten

Olive oil

Salt and pepper

To cook

Season and pan-fry the diced potato in a splash of olive oil over a medium heat for about 10 minutes until soft, then add the sliced leek and continue to pan-fry for another 5 minutes. Transfer to a bowl, add the Cheddar and mix everything together, crushing the potatoes slightly.

Line a rectangular dish approximately 10 x 5cm with cling film. Transfer the filling to the dish and squash it down with the back of a spoon. Refrigerate for about 1 hour until it sets into a block shape.

Preheat your oven to 190°C/gas mark 5.

Remove the block of filling from the dish and wrap it in the sheet of puff pastry. Place on a lined baking tray, brush with beaten egg and bake in the oven for about 30 minutes until golden brown, then serve.

ONION BIRYANI

Here, I slowly caramelise red onions to create a gorgeous sticky, sweet base to replace the meat in a typical biryani. Packed with flavour, this dish is a winner.

To make one portion

2 red onions, thinly sliced

½ tsp curry powder

½ vegetable stock cube

¼ mug of basmati rice

½ mug of water

Pinch of turmeric

Pinch of desiccated coconut

Olive oil

Salt and pepper

To cook

Preheat your oven to 190°C/gas mark 5.

Slowly pan-fry the onions in a splash of olive oil over a low-medium heat with a pinch of salt. After about 15 minutes, when the onions have started to caramelise, add the curry powder and crumble in the stock cube. Fry for a few more minutes, then transfer to an ovenproof dish.

Top with the rice, pour over the water and add the turmeric. Season then cover the dish tightly with a sheet of foil and bake in the oven for about 30 minutes until all the water has been absorbed by the rice and the rice is cooked. Sprinkle with the desiccated coconut and serve.

NASI GORENG

Toasted sesame oil is the key to this dish. Have a bottle of it in your kitchen and you'll be eating Asian food that tastes so authentic that you'll be amazed you made it in your own home.

To make one portion

½ mug of brown rice

1 mug of water

Wedge of Savoy cabbage, finely shredded

Sesame oil

½ carrot, cut into matchsticks

1 garlic clove, crushed

Soy sauce

1 egg

Squirt of sriracha

To cook

Put the rice and water in a saucepan and cook over a medium heat with the lid on for about 15 minutes, until all the water has been absorbed and the rice is cooked. Remove the lid and allow to cool.

Pan-fry the cabbage in a splash of sesame oil over a medium-high heat for a few minutes, then add the carrot. Fry for a few more minutes then add the cooled rice, crushed garlic, a splash of soy sauce and a splash more sesame oil. Fry for another 3 minutes and transfer to a plate or bowl.

Fry the egg in the pan then place it on top of the rice and finish with a squirt of sriracha.

PIL PIL PASTA

In Spain, we dunk bread into a delicious chilli- and garlic-infused oil, so I thought maybe a pasta dish using this philosophy would work nicely too. Pasta can be delicious simply dressed in olive oil, but the addition here of chilli, garlic and prawns is amazing.

To make one portion

150g linguine

1 garlic clove, sliced

Pinch of cayenne pepper or chilli powder

Pinch of dried chilli flakes or fresh sliced chilli

Handful of prawns, peeled (cooked or uncooked)

Pinch of chopped parsley

Olive oil

To cook

Cook the pasta in a pan of salted boiling water according to the packet instructions. Once cooked, drain and set aside.

Meanwhile, add a huge glug of olive oil to a cold frying pan. Add the garlic, then place over a medium heat and fry gently for a couple of minutes to infuse the oil with flavour, but not long enough to colour the garlic. Next add the cayenne pepper or chilli powder, along with the chilli flakes or fresh chilli. Stir, then add the prawns and fry for a couple more minutes.

Mix the pasta with the garlic and chilli oil and prawns, then garnish with the chopped parsley and serve.

GREEN BEANS & PESTO GNOCCHI

To make your pesto stretch further, you can 'water it down' by adding more olive oil. It's all about the ability to coat everything on the plate, and olive oil will help with that. Don't worry about diluting the flavour: trust me, you'll be able to taste the pesto just fine.

To make one portion

Handful of shop-bought gnocchi

Handful of green beans

2 tbsp pesto

Sprinkle of grated Parmesan cheese

Olive oil

Salt and pepper

To cook

Cook the gnocchi in a saucepan of salted boiling water according to the packet instructions. At the same time as you add the gnocchi to the saucepan, add the green beans too and cook together (the beans will take about 4 minutes to cook). Once cooked, drain.

Meanwhile, in a small bowl, mix the pesto with 2 tablespoons of olive oil. Stir this into the cooked gnocchi and beans. Garnish with lots of black pepper and a sprinkling of Parmesan, and serve.

PASTA ALLA NORMA

I had this at a restaurant called Norma and it was amazing! The humble aubergine is the star of this dish, which makes a delicious alternative to spaghetti bolognese. What better way to get more veg into your meal?

To make one portion

125g pasta of your choice

½ aubergine, roughly chopped

1 garlic clove, sliced

Pinch of dried chilli flakes

Pinch of dried oregano

200g chopped tomatoes (from a 400g tin)

Small handful of grated Parmesan cheese

Olive oil

Salt and pepper

To cook

Cook the pasta in a pan of salted boiling water according to the packet instructions. Once cooked, drain and save a little of the pasta water.

Meanwhile, pan-fry the chopped aubergine in a splash of olive oil over a medium heat for about 10 minutes. Add the garlic, oregano and chilli flakes, along with another splash of olive oil. Season with salt and pepper, then continue to cook for another few minutes until the garlic just starts to colour. Now add the chopped tomatoes and simmer for about 7 minutes.

Stir the cooked pasta into the sauce, adding a splash of the pasta water to loosen if needed. Serve with a scattering of Parmesan, a crack of black pepper and a little olive oil.

> **Tip** Use up the rest of the tinned tomatoes in one of my other recipes, like the Aubergine Parm Burger (page 181).

GNOCCHI SOUP

Dumplings are a great addition to soups, so why not gnocchi? I know it sounds strange, but it really does work brilliantly. If you don't want to blend the soup, just chop the onion extra small and make a chunkier, more rustic version.

To make one portion

½ onion, diced

1 garlic clove, diced

200g chopped tomatoes (from a 400g tin)

200ml water

½ vegetable stock cube

Handful of shop-bought gnocchi

Splash of single cream

Basil leaves, to serve (optional)

Olive oil

Salt and pepper

To cook

Pan-fry the onions in a splash of olive oil over a medium–low heat for about 7 minutes, seasoning with salt and pepper. Add the garlic and continue to fry for a few more minutes. Next, add the chopped tomatoes and water, and crumble in the stock cube. Simmer for about 10 minutes, adding an extra splash of water if it looks too thick. If it looks too watery, just simmer for a little longer.

Transfer the soup to a blender (or use a stick blender) and blend until smooth. Return to the pan, then add the gnocchi and simmer for another 3–5 minutes until the gnocchi is cooked through. Serve with a splash of cream and a few basil leaves, if you like.

BROCCOLI STEM FRIED RICE

Here's an idea for using up those chunky broccoli stalks: just chop them up to create broccoli 'rice' and stir-fry.

To make one portion

- ½ head of broccoli
- 1 garlic clove, sliced
- 2 spring onions, each cut into about 5 pieces
- ¼ carrot, cut into matchsticks
- 1 fresh red chilli, sliced (or a pinch of dried chilli flakes)
- Splash of soy sauce
- Sesame oil
- Salt and pepper

To cook

Chop the broccoli into florets and blitz in a food processor to form coarse chunks – they should be bigger than grains of rice. (If you don't have a food processor, you can chop the broccoli by hand with a knife or grate it.)

Pan-fry the garlic, spring onion, carrot and chilli in a splash of sesame oil over a high heat for a couple of minutes, or until the garlic just starts to colour. Add the chopped broccoli and continue to fry for 5–10 minutes, or until cooked. Season to taste, then transfer to a plate and add a splash of soy sauce before serving.

ASPARAGUS FRIED RICE WITH A CRISPY EGG

You can throw almost anything into fried rice and get amazing results, so why not asparagus? I like to dip asparagus in a runny egg yolk, so here, instead of scrambling the egg like you usually do with fried rice, I thought it might be nice to fry the egg and stick it on top.

To make one portion

- ¼ onion, finely diced
- 1 garlic clove, finely diced
- A few spears of asparagus, sliced into chunks at an angle
- Handful of leftover cold rice

- 1 tsp crispy chilli sauce, plus extra for garnish
- 1 egg
- Splash of soy sauce
- Vegetable oil

To cook

Pan-fry the onion in a splash of oil over a high heat for a couple of minutes before adding the garlic and asparagus. After about 2 minutes, as the garlic starts to colour, add the cooked rice and crispy chilli sauce, then continue to pan-fry for a few more minutes. Scrape everything to one side and crack an egg into the empty side. Fry the egg to your liking, then add a splash of soy sauce to the rice and give it a stir. Serve the rice with the fried egg on top, along with an extra dollop of crispy chilli sauce.

> Tip If you don't have any leftover rice, then simply pop ½ mug of rice and 1 mug of water in a saucepan with a lid. Cook over a medium heat for about 10 minutes, then allow to cool (you need to let it cool before frying or it will go mushy).

TOMATO POKE BOWL

This is a great way to use up old tomatoes: just chop them into cubes and pretend they are sushi-grade tuna. Although it doesn't taste like tuna, this poke recipe works great with most things. The sauce and rice can elevate anything, transforming it into a beautiful lunchtime treat.

To make one portion

¼ mug rice

½ mug water

1 tbsp sesame oil

2 tbsp soy sauce

1 tsp rice wine vinegar

1 garlic clove, grated

1cm piece of fresh root ginger, grated

1 big tomato

½ carrot, cut into strips using a potato peeler

Small handful of shredded red cabbage

Small handful of edamame beans

Pinch of sesame seeds

Salt

To cook

Put the rice and the water in a saucepan with a pinch of salt. Cover with a lid and place over a medium heat for about 7 minutes until all the water is absorbed and the rice is cooked. Fluff with a fork to separate the grains.

Meanwhile, mix together the sesame oil, soy sauce, rice wine vinegar, garlic and ginger in a bowl, then add the chopped tomato.

Assemble the poke bowl by first adding the rice, followed by the carrot, cabbage, tomato and edamame beans. Pour the remaining marinade over the top and garnish with a pinch of sesame seeds.

COURGETTE KOFTAS WITH RICE & TOMATO SALAD

I find Greek cuisine so fresh and vibrant – it's the perfect food to eat on a hot day. Here, I have come up with a great way to substitute meat for veg while keeping those great Greek flavours.

To make one portion

¼ mug rice

½ mug water

½ courgette, grated

2 tbsp chickpea flour

Pinch of ground cumin

1 tomato, diced

¼ red onion, sliced

Squeeze of lemon juice

Olive oil

Salt and pepper

To cook

Put the rice and the water in a saucepan with a pinch of salt. Cover with a lid and place over a medium heat for about 7 minutes until all the water is absorbed and the rice is cooked. Set aside.

Place the grated courgette in a bowl and stir in the chickpea flour, along with a pinch of salt and the cumin. Leave for 5 minutes, then mix again.

Pan-fry dollops of the courgette mixture in a splash of olive oil over a medium heat, cooking for a few minutes on each side to create the koftas.

Meanwhile, make the tomato salad by mixing together the tomatoes and red onion in a small bowl. Drizzle over some olive oil and a squeeze of lemon. Season to taste, then leave to sit for 5 minutes to let the flavours mingle.

Serve the koftas with the rice and tomato salad.

GREEN BEAN & LENTIL SALAD

With just a handful of ingredients, this is how to make something from nothing. If you want to make the pancakes really flaky, then there is a little bit of extra effort required to create those layers, but it's totally worth it.

To make one portion

1 small potato, cut into slices

1 egg

Small handful of green beans

4 tbsp olive oil

1 tbsp red wine vinegar

1 tsp Dijon mustard

100g cooked green lentils (from a 400g tin), drained

Salt and pepper

To cook

Start by boiling the potato slices in a pan of salted water. After a couple of minutes, add the egg and boil for exactly 6½ minutes. Put the egg into a bowl of cold water to stop the cooking process and throw the beans into the boiling water. After a couple of minutes, when the beans and potato slices are cooked, drain and set to one side.

To make the dressing, mix the olive oil with the red wine vinegar and Dijon mustard, then season with a pinch each of salt and pepper.

Mix the lentils with the green beans and potato slices. Peel the egg, cut it in half and add it to the salad, then dress with the Dijon dressing.

> **Make it vegan** To make this dish vegan, substitute the egg with tofu or simply leave it out altogether.

ROASTED BUTTERNUT SQUASH & BULGUR WHEAT

One butternut squash goes far, so it's important to have a few easy recipes up your sleeve to keep it exciting on day 3, 4 or even 5. This is a dish I love to cook – I really like the combination of bulgur wheat, parsley and salty feta with the slightly sweet squash.

To make one portion

A few slices of butternut squash (skin on)

Handful of bulgur wheat

Handful of chopped parsley

Small handful of crumbled feta

Olive oil

Salt and pepper

To cook

Preheat your oven to 190°C/gas mark 5.

Put the butternut squash in a roasting tray, drizzle with olive oil and season with a pinch each of salt and pepper, then roast in the oven for about 30 minutes until soft and cooked through.

Meanwhile, cook the bulgur wheat in a saucepan of salted boiling water for about 10 minutes until cooked, then drain. Mix the drained bulgur wheat in a bowl with the chopped parsley, top with the crumbled feta and serve with the roasted butternut squash.

CHEESY LEEK-STUFFED MUSHROOMS

Really quick and easy, this is a huge shortcut to some delicious food with only a few ingredients. The key to this dish is to use a fine grater to create a fluffy mound of Cheddar that will combine with a splash of cream to create a 'no-cook' cheesy paste. It's also a delicious way to use up any stale bread you have lying around.

To make one portion

- Small handful of finely grated Cheddar cheese
- Splash of single cream
- 2 portobello mushrooms
- Small handful of chopped stale bread
- A few thin slices of leek
- Handful of rocket
- Olive oil
- Black pepper

To cook

Preheat your oven to 180°C/gas mark 4. Place the finely grated Cheddar in a bowl, then use a fork to mix in the cream. You want to create a paste similar in consistency to mashed potato.

Place the mushrooms on a baking tray and brush them all over with oil. Stuff with the cheese paste, then squash some small chunks of stale bread into the cheese. Top with some very thinly sliced leek, then brush the tops with a little more oil and sprinkle over some cracked black pepper. Bake in the oven for about 20 minutes, or until the tops start to brown and the mushrooms are cooked through. Serve with a handful of rocket.

> **Swap** Feel free to swap the Cheddar for whatever cheese you have in the fridge – and if you don't have leeks, spring onions will work well too.

SAUTÉED MUSHROOM COUSCOUS

Pan-fried mushrooms have a gorgeous nutty flavour and dark colour that, when paired with red onion and spinach, creates a more wintry vibe. Here I have added couscous to make a lovely one pan meal with very minimal effort but maximum impact on the plate.

To make one portion

Handful of mushrooms, sliced

½ red onion, sliced

Handful of spinach

1 egg-cup of couscous

1 egg-cup of water

Olive oil

Salt and pepper

To cook

Pan-fry the mushrooms and red onion together in a splash of olive oil over a medium heat. After about 10 minutes, once the mushrooms are dark in colour, add the spinach, a splash more oil, season with salt and pepper and wilt in the pan for a minute. Remove from the heat, and while the pan is still hot, throw in the couscous, then add the water, give it a quick stir and set the pan aside for a few minutes. Once the couscous plumps up it's ready to serve.

CORONATION CHICKPEAS

The texture of oven-roasted chickpeas makes them so delicious and moreish. One of my favourite ways to roast them is in a splash of olive oil and some curry powder, as I've done here.

To make one portion

- 200g chickpeas (from a 400g tin), drained
- 1 tsp curry powder for the chickpeas, plus ½ tsp for the sauce
- ½ mug of basmati rice
- 1 mug of water
- Pinch of ground turmeric
- Small handful of chopped coriander
- 2 tbsp crème fraîche
- Small handful of flaked almonds
- Olive oil
- Salt and pepper

To cook

Preheat your oven to 190°C/gas mark 5.

Put the chickpeas into an ovenproof dish and add a generous glug of olive oil, a teaspoon of curry powder and a pinch of salt and pepper. Mix and then roast in the oven for about 25 minutes until golden brown.

Meanwhile, put the rice, water and a pinch of turmeric into a saucepan and cook over a medium heat with the lid on for about 7 minutes until all the water is absorbed and the rice is cooked. Then fluff the rice with a fork and mix in the chopped coriander.

To make the sauce, mix the crème fraîche with half a teaspoon of curry powder and a pinch each of salt and pepper.

Serve the rice with a dollop of the sauce, topped with the chickpeas and garnished with flaked almonds.

FRIDGE-RAIDER FEASTS

PEAS, PASTA & CREAM

This is such a simple dish but it looks quite cool and is packed with so much flavour from the pepper and Parmesan in the sauce. It doesn't really matter which pasta shape you use here.

To make one portion

Handful of pasta

Handful of frozen peas

2 spring onions, roughly chopped

150ml single cream

Handful of grated Parmesan cheese, plus extra to serve

Olive oil

Salt and pepper

To cook

Cook the pasta in a pan of salted boiling water as per the instructions on the packet, adding the peas a few minutes before the end. Then drain, reserving some of the pasta cooking water for the sauce.

While the pasta is cooking, pan-fry the spring onions in a splash of olive oil over a medium heat for a few minutes until soft, then add the cream and simmer for 1 minute. Remove from the heat, stir in the Parmesan and season with salt and pepper. Add the pasta and the peas, along with a few tablespoons of the pasta water, and mix together. Serve with an extra sprinkle of Parmesan and a drizzle of olive oil.

FETA GOUJONS

I came up with this dish while I was experimenting with making feta goujons and chips. The goujons just worked better as a posh salad with roasted cherry tomatoes – perfect for a summer's day.

To make one portion

- 100g feta, cut into slices
- 1 tbsp plain flour
- 1 egg, beaten
- Small handful of breadcrumbs (grated stale bread)
- Small handful of cherry tomatoes
- Handful of rocket
- Olive oil
- Salt and pepper

To cook

Preheat your oven to 190°C/gas mark 5.

Dust the feta slices with plain flour, dip them in the beaten egg and then roll them in the breadcrumbs.

Place on a lined baking tray and cook in the oven for about 25 minutes until golden brown. Place the tomatoes in an ovenproof dish, add a splash of olive oil and a pinch each of salt and pepper, then cook in the oven for about 15 minutes until soft and gooey.

When the feta goujons and tomatoes are cooked, serve them hot on a handful of rocket.

> **Make it vegan** To make this dish vegan, substitute the feta for a plant-based Greek-style cheese. Substitute the egg by brushing the cheese with a little oil before dipping in the breadcrumbs (no need to dust with flour).

TIKKA HALLOUMI

I like the tasty charred bits you get on chicken tikka cooked in a tandoor oven, but it's actually quite difficult to achieve this effect with normal home appliances. So, I tried recreating it with halloumi instead, as it's cheese that takes on colour well. It worked brilliantly, so now you can make your own perfectly charred tikka – and there's no need for chicken, so it's meat-free.

To make one portion

½ mug rice

1 mug water

Pinch of ground turmeric

A few slices of halloumi

1 tsp curry powder

Shop-bought crispy fried onions (or fry your own)

Handful of chopped coriander

Olive oil

Salt

To cook

Put the rice, water and turmeric in a saucepan with a pinch of salt. Cover with a lid and place over a medium heat for about 7 minutes until all the water is absorbed and the rice is cooked.

Meanwhile coat the halloumi in oil and curry powder, then pan-fry over a medium heat for a few minutes on each side until nicely charred.

Serve with the rice and garnish with crispy fried onions and coriander.

GRATED HALLOUMI FAJITAS

If you grate halloumi, it goes so much further, giving you little crumbs of salty cheese that are perfect for these simple fajitas. Be sure not to add any salt: the halloumi is all you need here.

To make one portion

50g halloumi, grated

½ red onion, sliced

½ green pepper, sliced

Pinch of ground cumin

Pinch of paprika

A few tortillas

Dollop of crème fraîche

A few cherry tomatoes, quartered

Small handful of coriander (optional)

Pepper

Olive oil

To cook

Start by pan-frying the grated halloumi for a few minutes in a dry pan over a medium heat. Transfer to a plate and set aside, then return the pan to the heat and pan-fry the onion and green pepper in a splash of olive oil for 5 minutes. Season with pepper and sprinkle over the paprika and cumin – remember, there's no need for salt.

Gently heat the tortillas in a clean frying pan over a low heat, just to soften them up, then divide the onions and peppers between them. Top with the grated halloumi, then a little crème fraîche, a few tomato quarters and some coriander. Roll up and enjoy.

> **Tip** For something more substantial, add half a can of chickpeas or black beans to the pan when you're cooking the onion and pepper.

HALLOUMI CAESAR SALAD

Cooking halloumi in the oven creates a beautiful caramelisation that sort of reminds me of chicken and makes it a great alternative. The croutons in this salad add extra crunch and are a great way of using up stale bread.

To make one portion

100g halloumi, sliced

A few chunks of old sourdough bread

Pinch of dried oregano

1 tbsp mayonnaise

1 tsp Dijon mustard

A few lettuce leaves

Sprinkling of grated Parmesan cheese

Olive oil

Pepper

To cook

Preheat your oven to 180°C/gas mark 4.

Drizzle the halloumi slices with olive oil and season with pepper and oregano (you don't need salt as halloumi is already salty). Spread out on a baking tray and roast for about 15 minutes until slightly browned. Halfway through the cooking time, add the bread to the tray and turn the halloumi.

Meanwhile, in a small bowl, mix together the mayonnaise and mustard with 3 tablespoons of olive oil to create a smooth dressing. Arrange the lettuce in a serving bowl and top with the halloumi and toasted sourdough croutons. Drizzle over some dressing and finish with some grated Parmesan and cracked black pepper.

CRISPY POTATO CAESAR SALAD

Crisp up those potatoes to get them extra crunchy and add this quick homemade Caesar dressing to create my tasty £1 version of a Caesar salad that doesn't compromise on flavour.

To make one portion

- A few small potatoes, skin on
- 1 tbsp red wine vinegar
- 1 tbsp mayonnaise
- Pinch of dried oregano
- A few lettuce leaves
- Olive oil
- Salt and pepper

To cook

Preheat your oven to 190°C/gas mark 5.

Cook the potatoes in a pan of salted boiling water for about 15 minutes until soft and cooked. Drain and let them steam for a bit to dry out.

Transfer the potatoes to an ovenproof dish and squash each one slightly with the back of a fork to break the skins and expose the fluffy middle. Pour over a generous glug of olive oil, add a pinch of salt and roast for about 40 minutes until crispy.

Meanwhile, to make the dressing, mix together 5 tablespoons of olive oil with the red wine vinegar, mayo, oregano, and a pinch each of salt and pepper. Stir with a fork to combine the ingredients into a creamy sauce, then serve with the lettuce and potatoes.

> **Make it vegan** To make this dish vegan, substitute the mayo with vegan mayo.

ROTOLO

Real Italian rotolo is complicated to make – it even has a crazy step where you have to wrap the pasta in a cloth and boil it. I wanted to eat it, but I didn't want to make it, so I had to come up with my own One Pound Meals formula. Here it is.

To make one portion

- 3 tbsp ricotta
- 2 small handfuls of grated Parmesan
- Small handful of spinach
- 1 fresh lasagne sheet

- Big glug of single cream
- Small handful of frozen peas
- Olive oil
- Salt and pepper

To cook

Preheat your oven to 190°C/gas mark 5.

Mix the ricotta with half the grated Parmesan, the spinach (you don't need to wilt the spinach, it will soften as you mix it) and a pinch of salt and pepper. Spread the mixture evenly over the sheet of fresh pasta, then roll the pasta into a sausage shape.

Cut the rolled-up pasta sheet into 2.5cm-thick circles and place in an ovenproof dish cut side up. Add the cream, peas and remaining handful of Parmesan to the dish along with a splash of water, drizzle with olive oil and season with salt and pepper. Bake in the oven for about 15 minutes, then serve.

MILK RISOTTO

A while ago, I was curious to find out if you could make risotto with milk. It turns out that it tastes amazing, and adding a pinch of tarragon takes it to a whole new level of deliciousness. But the biggest revelation about my experiment was discovering that plant-based milk makes a super-creamy vegan risotto.

To make one portion

½ onion, diced

Handful of arborio rice

300ml milk

Pinch of dried tarragon

A few asparagus spears, cut into thin strips with a potato peeler

Olive oil

Salt and pepper

To cook

Gently pan-fry the onion in a splash of olive oil over a low-medium heat for about 5 minutes, until softened but not coloured. Season with salt and pepper then turn up the heat to medium and add the rice. Stir to coat the rice in the oil, then start adding the milk little by little, about 50ml at a time, while stirring continuously. After 10–15 minutes, once all the milk is added and the rice is cooked, remove the pan from the heat, stir in the tarragon, season to taste and top with the asparagus and a splash of olive oil.

> **Make it vegan** To make this dish vegan, use a plant-based milk.

WATERMELON & FETA SALAD

Fresh and vibrant, this watermelon salad is perfect for when the weather gets hot and you need cooling down. There's no cooking required – just chuck everything in a bowl and serve.

To make one portion

- 1 slice of watermelon, chopped into cubes
- A few chunks of feta cheese
- ¼ cucumber, roughly chopped
- A few very thin slices of red onion
- 6 fresh mint leaves, 3 chopped and 3 left whole
- Drizzle of balsamic glaze
- Olive oil
- Salt and pepper

To cook

Simply place the watermelon, feta, cucumber, onion and chopped mint in a bowl. Season and toss to combine, then dress with a drizzle of olive oil and the balsamic glaze. Serve topped with the whole mint leaves.

> **Tip** This is easy to scale up to serve more people, so it's perfect for a summer barbecue. It also makes a great packed lunch on a hot day.

FILO BIANCO

This thin and crispy tart is packed with flavour. And the oozy filling works so well with the brittle edges of the filo pastry, creating a lovely contrast in texture. But my favourite thing about this dish is the tiny splashes of Worcestershire sauce that cut through the richness of the cheese and cream.

To make one portion

- 3 sheets of filo pastry
- Handful of grated Cheddar cheese
- Splash of single cream
- A few Tenderstem broccoli florets
- Splash of Worcestershire sauce
- Olive oil
- Pinch of black pepper

To cook

Preheat your oven to 190°C/gas mark 5.

Grab a 12cm heatproof dish or a small frying pan with an oven-proof handle and lay the sheets of filo in the dish or pan so that they overlap in the middle and overhang around the sides of the dish. Scrunch the edges up to create a circular pie case that will contain a filling, and brush lightly with olive oil.

Mix the cheese and single cream in a bowl with the pepper to create a paste, then spoon into the filo pastry case. Top with the broccoli florets, add a few splashes of Worcestershire sauce and bake in the oven for about 20 minutes until the pastry is golden brown.

CARAMELISED ONION QUICHE

Onions bring so much depth of flavour to a dish like this. They are my number-one ingredient for adding oomph when cooking on a budget. Just fry them slowly and the natural sugars start to caramelise, creating a tasty filling for your quiche.

To make one portion

- 1 red onion, sliced
- 20 x 20cm square of shop-bought shortcrust pastry
- 3 eggs
- Splash of milk
- Small handful of grated Cheddar cheese
- Olive oil
- Salt and pepper

To cook

Preheat your oven to 190°C/gas mark 5.

Season and pan-fry the onion gently in a splash of olive oil over a low-medium heat for about 10 to 15 minutes, until it starts to caramelise.

Remove the pan from the heat and allow the onion to cool while you line a round ovenproof dish about 15cm in diameter with the shortcrust pastry. Trim the edges to make a neat pastry case, then prepare your filling.

Crack the eggs into a bowl, add the milk, caramelised onion, grated cheese and a pinch each of salt and pepper. Pour the filling mixture into the pastry-lined dish and bake in the oven for about 20 minutes until the filling is set and golden brown on top.

CREAMY CAULIFLOWER TAGLIATELLE

Cooking the cauliflower two ways for this dish gives it contrasting textures and tastes, making it seem way more complicated than it actually is.

To make one portion

- ½ cauliflower, chopped into chunks
- 1 mug of almond milk
- Handful of dried tagliatelle
- Olive oil
- Salt and pepper

To cook

Keep some nice-looking small cauliflower florets to one side for the topping.

Bring a pan of salted water to the boil, add the cauliflower chunks and cook for about 10 minutes until soft.

Drain the cauliflower then blitz in a food processor, along with the mug of almond milk and a generous pinch of salt and pepper, until smooth.

Meanwhile, season and pan-fry the florets in a glug of olive oil over a medium heat for about 6 minutes, and cook the pasta in a pan of salted boiling water until al dente.

Drain the pasta and mix it with the cauliflower sauce, transfer to a plate, top with the pan-fried florets, drizzle with a generous glug of olive oil, and season with salt and pepper to serve.

CIABATTA ALFREDO

My inspiration for this dish was my love of using a piece of bread to mop up those delicious flavours at the end of a meal. You can use any bread, but I chose ciabatta because it makes the whole thing sound more Italian.

To make one portion

125g tagliatelle

2 garlic cloves, crushed or grated

A few slices of ciabatta

200ml single cream

Handful of grated Parmesan cheese

Handful of chopped parsley

Olive oil

Salt and pepper

To cook

Preheat your oven to 180°C/gas mark 4.

Cook the tagliatelle in a pan of salted boiling water according to the packet instructions. Once cooked, drain and save a little of the pasta water.

Meanwhile, add a generous glug of olive oil to a cold pan along with the crushed garlic and place over a medium heat. Just as the garlic begins to fry (but before it starts to colour), dip each of the ciabatta slices into the pan, then transfer to a baking tray. Place in the oven and leave to cook for 5–10 minutes until crispy and slightly charred at the edges.

Add the cream to the remaining garlic-infused oil in the pan and simmer for a few minutes, then remove from the heat. Season, then add the Parmesan and half of the parsley. Stir in the cooked pasta and a splash of the pasta cooking water, then mix in the toasted ciabatta slices and serve with the remaining parsley as a garnish.

CACIO E PEPE

A traditional cacio e pepe uses a pasta called bucatini, but really any pasta will do. I spent ages trying to find bucatini and it was a complete nightmare. Spaghetti works just as well and I'm sure no one will notice.

To make one portion

125g spaghetti

3 tbsp butter

Small handful of grated Parmesan cheese

Salt and pepper

To cook

Cook the pasta in a pan of boiling salted water as per the instructions on the packet, then drain, reserving some of the pasta cooking water.

Heat the butter in a pan over a medium heat until it starts bubbling, then add a few tablespoons of the pasta water while stirring continuously. After a couple of minutes remove from the heat and add the grated Parmesan and loads of black pepper, stirring for a few minutes until the sauce thickens a little. Add the cooked pasta, mix well, then serve.

ROCKET & PARMESAN SOUP

An easy-peasy soup that has a nice peppery taste thanks to the rocket, and a savoury edge from the cheese. It's great for using up wilted rocket and those leftover ends of Parmesan.

To make one portion

1 slice of stale bread

½ onion, diced

2 mugs of water

1 vegetable stock cube

Handful of rocket

Handful of grated Parmesan, plus a few shavings to garnish

Olive oil

Salt and pepper

To cook

Drizzle the bread with olive oil and sprinkle over some salt, then toast under a hot grill or in a griddle pan over a medium heat. Chop into squares and set aside.

Meanwhile, fry the onion in a splash of olive oil in a saucepan over a medium heat for about 5 minutes until it just starts to colour.

Chuck in the water, along with the stock cube, rocket and grated Parmesan. Bring to a simmer and let it bubble away for a couple of minutes. Transfer to a blender and blitz until smooth, then season to taste. Serve in a bowl with a garnish of shaved Parmesan and a drizzle of olive oil, with the croutons scattered over the top.

> **Tip** Add the Parmesan rind to the pan while cooking for extra flavour and scoop it out before you blend the soup.

PORTOBELLO STILTON BURGER

This is so simple to make. Just crumble some Stilton onto a mushroom, bake it, and there you have it: my quick and easy veggie burger. The potatoes become sort of like nuggets when they're cooked and are a perfect accompaniment.

To make one portion

A few small potatoes, skin on

1 portobello mushroom

Small handful of Stilton

1 bread bun, toasted

A few lettuce leaves

Squeeze of tomato ketchup

Olive oil

Salt

To cook

Preheat your oven to 190°C/gas mark 5.

Cook the potatoes in a pan of salted boiling water for about 15 minutes until soft. Drain and let them steam for a bit to dry out.

Transfer the potatoes to an ovenproof dish and squash each one slightly with the back of a fork to break the skin and expose the fluffy middle. Pour over a generous glug of olive oil, add a pinch of salt and roast for about 40 minutes until crispy.

When the potatoes have about 15 minutes of cooking time left, brush the outside of the mushroom with olive oil, turn it upside down and crumble the Stilton into it. Place on a baking tray and cook for about 15 minutes in the oven until the mushroom is cooked and the cheese has totally melted.

Serve the mushroom burger in a toasted bun with a few lettuce leaves alongside the crispy potatoes and a ketchup dip.

GREEN VEG TOAD IN THE HOLE

I saw some mini leeks and courgettes in the supermarket and thought they'd be great for this dish, but you can easily use normal-sized veg and just chop it into chunks.

To make one portion

40g plain flour

1 large egg

60ml milk

2 mini leeks

2 mini courgettes

Handful of frozen peas

1 tbsp gravy granules

Salt and pepper

Olive oil

To cook

Preheat your oven to 180°C/gas mark 4.

Pour some oil into an ovenproof dish to a depth of about 1cm. Place in the oven to heat for roughly 10 minutes until the oil is smoking hot.

Meanwhile, to make the batter, mix the flour, egg and milk in a bowl with a pinch of salt. Very carefully, remove the hot dish from the oven and add the leeks and courgettes. Pour the batter into the dish and immediately return it to the oven. Bake for about 20–30 minutes until everything has risen perfectly and is a lovely golden brown colour. Don't open the oven door to check for at least the first 15 minutes.

Meanwhile, cook the peas in a pan of boiling salted water over a medium heat for about 3 minutes, then drain. Make the gravy according to the packet instructions. Serve the veggie toad in the hole with the peas, with gravy poured over the top.

> **Swap** This recipe will work well with most vegetables, so it's a great way of using up any different leftover veg you have.

CAULIFLOWER LARB LETTUCE CUPS

A lovely summer dish, and easy to scale up to enjoy with friends: just place a big bowlful in the middle of the table and everyone can dig in and make their own lettuce wraps. Larb is usually made with meat, but here I've swapped it for tiny cauliflower florets for a veg-based version that's just as tasty.

To make one portion

½ red onion, finely diced

¼ head of cauliflower, chopped into small florets

1 garlic clove, grated or crushed

Pinch of dried chilli flakes

Pinch of curry powder

A few lettuce leaves

Handful of chopped coriander

½ lime

Olive oil

Salt and pepper

To cook

Season the onion and cauliflower, then pan-fry in a splash of olive oil over a medium heat for about 6 minutes. Add the garlic, chilli flakes and curry powder, and continue to fry for a few more minutes until everything is golden brown.

Spoon the mixture into lettuce leaves, then garnish with chopped coriander and squeeze over some lime before serving.

CHARRED SWEETCORN & SALSA WITH BULGUR WHEAT

This one is all about that charred flavour you get from cooking a whole sweetcorn on the hob, so don't be afraid to get a little smoky. It's a great way of using sweetcorn straight from the farm, and is a perfect recipe for using up overripe tomatoes.

To make one portion

Handful of bulgur wheat

1 vegetable stock cube

1 sweetcorn cob

1 tomato, diced

2 spring onions, sliced

Squirt of sriracha sauce

1 tbsp crème fraîche

Pinch of smoked paprika

Olive oil

Salt and pepper

To cook

Place the bulgur wheat in a saucepan of boiling water and crumble in the stock cube. Cook for about 10 minutes until the bulgur wheat is cooked through, then drain.

Meanwhile, place the corn in a saucepan over a high heat and cook for a minute or two on each side to cook through and create some charring. Once cooked, carefully slice down the length of the corn cob to separate the sweetcorn kernels into strips.

In a small bowl, combine the tomato, spring onion and sriracha with a splash of olive oil to make a spicy salsa. Season to taste, then set to one side.

In a serving bowl, combine the charred sweetcorn and bulgur wheat. Add the salsa, then top with the crème fraîche and sprinkle over the smoked paprika.

SAUSAGE & BLACK BEAN STIR-FRY

You wouldn't usually think about using sausage in a stir-fry but, when you complement it with black beans, garlic and soy sauce, you get an exceptional depth of flavour that makes this dish a taste explosion.

To make one portion

- 2 sausages
- Sesame oil
- 1 garlic clove, sliced
- A few dried chillies (or dried chilli flakes)
- 200g black beans (from a 400g tin), drained
- Splash of soy sauce
- Handful of green beans
- Salt and pepper

To cook

Cut the sausage skins, squeeze out the meat and pan-fry it in a splash of sesame oil over a medium heat, breaking it up into chunks with a wooden spoon, for about 5 minutes. When the sausage meat starts to brown, throw in the garlic and continue to fry for a few minutes. When the garlic starts to brown, add the dried chillies, black beans, soy sauce, green beans and a splash of water. Simmer for about 4 minutes until the beans are soft and the sauce has reduced slightly. Remove from the heat, season with salt and pepper, a splash more soy sauce if required, and a tiny drizzle of sesame oil, then serve.

SPEEDY SUPPERS

GREEN MAC & CHEESE

Here's an easy way to eat more veggies using frozen spinach. There's no extra cooking required: it just defrosts in the pan. I've even added some green to the crispy breadcrumb topping.

To make one portion

Handful of macaroni

1 tsp butter

1 tsp plain flour

200ml milk

3 discs of frozen spinach

Handful of grated Cheddar cheese

Handful of breadcrumbs

Handful of finely chopped parsley

1 garlic clove, crushed

Olive oil

Salt and pepper

To cook

Cook the macaroni in a pan of boiling salted water according to the packet instructions. Once cooked, drain, then drizzle with olive oil and set aside until needed.

Meanwhile, melt the butter in a saucepan over a medium heat. Stir in the flour and cook for a few minutes, then add the milk, a little at a time, stirring continuously. Once the mixture has formed a sauce, add the frozen spinach and stir until defrosted. Remove from the heat and add the cheese, stirring until it melts into the sauce. Now stir in the drained pasta, then season to taste and transfer to an ovenproof dish (you can stir in an extra splash of milk if it needs loosening).

In a small bowl, mix together the breadcrumbs, parsley and crushed garlic, and season with a pinch of salt and pepper. Add a glug of olive oil, then sprinkle the breadcrumb mixture over the mac and cheese. Bake for about 15 minutes, or until the breadcrumbs are nicely toasted, then serve.

BLACK OLIVE PESTO WITH SPAGHETTI

Pesto is expensive because it contains premium ingredients, so here is an easy alternative using a jar of black olives. These are great because they are packed with a powerful and distinct flavour.

To make one portion

125g spaghetti

Handful of black olives, plus a few extra, halved, to garnish

Handful of rocket

Small handful of grated Parmesan, plus extra to serve

Olive oil

Salt and pepper

To cook

Cook the spaghetti in a pan of salted boiling water according to the packet instructions, then drain.

Meanwhile, place the olives, rocket and Parmesan in a food processor, along with a big glug of olive oil, and blitz to make a paste. Loosen with loads more olive oil and season to taste.

Mix the cooked pasta with the black olive pesto, then serve, garnished with a little more Parmesan, some halved black olives, an extra drizzle of olive oil and some cracked black pepper.

> **Tip** This black olive pesto is also great on toast as a tapenade. You could also stir it into soup or drizzle it over fried eggs.

GNOCCHI POMODORO

This recipe is all about using up that leftover cheese in the fridge: the more the better, and don't be afraid of mixing. Here I've added a bit of Stilton along with a little Cheddar, for a dramatic depth of flavour.

To make one portion

- 200g chopped tomatoes (from a 400g tin)
- Handful of shop-bought gnocchi
- Handful of grated Cheddar cheese
- A few small chunks of Stilton
- 1 tsp dried oregano
- Olive oil
- Salt and pepper

To cook

Preheat your oven to 180°C/gas mark 4.

Grab an ovenproof dish and add the chopped tomatoes and gnocchi. Add some of the grated Cheddar and chunks of Stilton, then season with salt, pepper and oregano. Give it a little stir, then scatter over the rest of the cheese and drizzle with olive oil. Bake for about 35 minutes and serve.

> **Swap** You can use whatever kind of cheese you like.

VEGGIE SAUSAGE PASTA

A great swap for a greener meal is to replace regular sausages with veggie ones: they are packed with flavour. Here's an easy recipe for you to try. This is also a great recipe for using up those last bits of pasta in the packet – you can combine different shapes, so you never need to let any go to waste.

To make one portion

Big handful of any pasta

2 veggie sausages, sliced into 1cm slices

1 courgette, roughly chopped

1 tbsp red pesto

Olive oil

Salt and pepper

To cook

Cook the pasta in a pan of salted boiling water according to the packet instructions. Once cooked, drain and save a little of the pasta water.

Pan-fry the veggie sausages and courgette in a splash of olive oil over a medium heat for about 10 minutes until cooked through. Then add the pasta, along with the red pesto and a splash of cooking water. Season to taste and serve.

> **Swap** This will work well with most veg – try throwing in a handful of frozen peas if you don't have a courgette.

MESSY PEA LASAGNE

This is a super-speedy meal made from just three ingredients; it can be cobbled together at a moment's notice. The goat's cheese gives it a lovely depth of flavour and the crispy lasagne sheet adds texture to this very simple dish.

To make one portion

Handful of frozen peas

Handful of crumbled goat's cheese

1 dried lasagne sheet

Olive oil

Salt and pepper

To cook

Preheat the grill to high.

Put the frozen peas into a pan of boiling water, and as soon as the water starts to boil again, remove from the heat and drain. Transfer to an ovenproof dish, season with salt and pepper, then scatter over half the crumbled goat's cheese.

Soften the lasagne sheet in a bowl of boiling water for a few minutes. Lay the lasagne sheet on top of the peas and goat's cheese, folding it in half, then add the remaining goat's cheese. Season with another pinch each of salt and pepper, then drizzle with olive oil.

Cook under the grill for about 5 minutes until the lasagne sheet has turned golden brown at the edges, then serve.

SPEEDY CHORIZO BOLOGNESE

Pan-fried chorizo goes so well with a tangy tomato passata. As the sauce bubbles away, the tomato flavours intensify and mix with the spicy paprika-infused oil from the chorizo to create a totally different style of bolognese. And, thanks to all these strong flavours, this lovely rich and intense sauce can be made in just minutes.

To make one portion

Handful of dried tagliatelle pasta

A few slices of cooking chorizo

2 spring onions, roughly sliced

200g passata

Olive oil

Salt and pepper

To cook

Bring a pan of salted water to the boil and cook the tagliatelle until al dente.

Meanwhile, pan-fry the chorizo slices in a glug of olive oil over a medium heat for a few minutes until they start to colour. Add the spring onions and continue to fry for a further minute before adding the passata. Season well with salt and pepper, add another glug of olive oil and simmer for a few more minutes until the sauce is reduced.

Serve the sauce with the pasta and sprinkle with cracked black pepper.

CAPER PUTTANESCA

Using the brine from a jar of capers is what makes this dish so special. Something that would ordinarily be thrown away actually has the ability to transform this into one of my favourite pasta dishes.

To make one portion

- 2 garlic cloves, sliced
- 2 pinches of dried chilli flakes
- 200g chopped tomatoes (from a 400g tin)
- Small handful of capers, plus a splash of caper brine
- Small handful of pitted black olives
- Handful of dried spaghetti
- Olive oil
- Salt and pepper

To cook

Pan-fry the garlic and a pinch of the chilli flakes in a generous glug of olive oil over a medium heat for about 3 minutes until the garlic starts to brown. Add the chopped tomatoes, capers, caper brine and olives, season to taste with salt and pepper, then simmer for about 10 minutes.

Meanwhile, bring a pan of salted water to the boil and cook the spaghetti until al dente.

Use tongs to transfer the spaghetti to the sauce, along with a couple of tablespoons of the cooking water, and mix it all together. Sprinkle with the remaining pinch of chilli flakes and drizzle with a glug of olive oil to serve.

SPRING ONION NOODLES

Spring onions are the most important part of any noodle dish: they provide that all important depth of flavour. So, how about a noodle dish with triple the spring onions?! This is a great dish to whip up for a quick meal, and most of the ingredients will already be in your storecupboard.

To make one portion

6 spring onions

1 garlic clove, crushed

1 red chilli (or a pinch of chilli flakes), sliced

1 nest of your favourite kind of noodles

Sprinkle of gravy granules (or ⅛ stock cube, crumbled)

Splash of soy sauce

Sesame oil

Salt

To cook

Chop your spring onions randomly so the pieces are different sizes. Season with salt and pepper, then pan-fry, along with the garlic and chilli, in a splash of olive oil over a medium heat for a few minutes.

Meanwhile, cook the noodles in a pan of boiling water according to the packet instructions. Once cooked, use tongs to transfer the noodles to the frying pan containing the spring onions, garlic and chilli (you want the noodles to still be a bit wet). Sprinkle over the gravy granules and a splash of soy sauce, then mix well and serve.

> **Tip** This is the perfect dish for using up any veggie scraps you have kicking around in the fridge – just fry them up with the spring onions and enjoy.

TOFU & BROCCOLI STIR-FRY

This super-quick stir-fry is spicy but also sticky and sweet, and is accompanied perfectly with a side of fluffy basmati rice.

To make one portion

½ mug of basmati rice

1 mug of water

A few stems of broccoli

Sesame oil

100g firm tofu, cubed

1 garlic clove, sliced

Squirt of sriracha

Splash of passata

1 tbsp golden syrup

Soy sauce

Pinch of dried chilli flakes

Pinch of sesame seeds

Salt and pepper

To cook

Put the rice and water in a saucepan and cook over a medium heat with the lid on for about 7 minutes. When all the water has been absorbed and the rice is cooked, turn off the heat, remove the lid and fluff up the rice with a fork.

Meanwhile, pan-fry the broccoli in a splash of sesame oil over a medium heat for a few minutes then add the tofu and garlic. Season with salt and pepper and cook for a few more minutes until the garlic starts to colour.

Add the sriracha, passata, golden syrup, a splash of soy sauce and the chilli flakes and cook for a further few minutes until the sauce has thickened.

Serve the tofu and broccoli with the rice, garnished with sesame seeds.

FRIED CAULIFLOWER RICE

The cornerstones of my Chinese cuisine shortcuts are garlic, sesame oil and soy sauce. With these three ingredients, anyone can turn a few vegetables into a Friday night takeaway.

To make one portion

- ¼ cauliflower, finely chopped into rice-size pieces
- Sesame oil
- 1 garlic clove, sliced
- ½ carrot, cut into matchsticks
- 1 spring onion, roughly chopped
- Handful of frozen broad beans, shelled
- Soy sauce
- Pinch of sesame seeds
- Salt and pepper

To cook

Season the cauliflower with salt and pepper and pan-fry it in a splash of sesame oil over a medium heat for about 5 minutes until soft and cooked through.

Meanwhile, in a separate pan over a medium heat, fry the garlic, carrot and spring onion in a splash of sesame oil for about 5 minutes until the garlic starts to brown, adding the shelled broad beans and a splash of soy sauce about halfway through.

Mix everything together in a bowl then garnish with sesame seeds and another splash of soy sauce.

VEGAN LENTIL CHILLI

Chilli is a great idea for a social occasion. One big pot in the middle of the table makes for a casual and relaxed catch-up with friends and family.

To make one portion ··

½ red onion, sliced

1 garlic clove, sliced

Handful of Puy lentils

1 tsp ground cumin

200g chopped tomatoes (from a 400g tin)

1 mug of water for the chilli, plus 1 mug for the rice

1 vegetable stock cube

100g kidney beans (from a 400g tin), drained

½ mug of basmati rice

Small handful of chopped coriander

Olive oil

Salt and pepper

To cook ··

Grab a saucepan and fry the onion and garlic in a splash of olive oil over a medium heat. After about 5 minutes, just as the garlic is starting to brown, add the Puy lentils, a teaspoon of cumin, the chopped tomatoes, a mug of water and the stock cube. Season then simmer for about 10–15 minutes until the lentils are cooked and the sauce has reduced to a thicker consistency. About 5 minutes before the end of the cooking time, add the drained kidney beans.

Meanwhile, put the rice and a mug of water into a saucepan and cook over a medium heat with the lid on for about 7 minutes until all the water has been absorbed and the rice is cooked. Fluff with a fork and stir in some chopped coriander, then serve with the chilli.

PULLED CHICKEN & BLACK BEAN CHILLI

Replacing beef with chicken is a small step in the right direction when it comes to reducing your impact on the environment. This tasty chilli is great for a midweek meal.

To make one portion

- 1 chicken leg
- ½ red onion, sliced
- 1 garlic clove
- 1 tsp smoked paprika
- 1 tsp ground cumin
- 200g chopped tomatoes (from a 400g tin)
- 1 veg, chicken or beef stock cube
- 200g black beans (from a 400g tin), drained
- Dollop of crème fraîche
- A few coriander leaves (optional)
- A few slices of red chilli (optional)
- Olive oil
- Salt and pepper

To cook

Season the chicken leg and place it in a saucepan or casserole dish with a splash of olive oil over a medium heat. Add the onion and cook for about 10 minutes until the chicken is coloured on all sides. Next add the garlic, paprika and cumin, and continue to fry for a couple more minutes before adding the chopped tomatoes and the stock cube. Stir to combine, then cover with a lid and simmer for about 25 minutes, adding a splash of water if required.

Remove the chicken from the sauce and place on a plate. Use a fork to shred the meat. Discard the bone and return the meat to the saucepan. Add the black beans to the pan and simmer for another couple of minutes.

Season to taste and serve with a dollop of crème fraîche, and a few coriander leaves and slices of chilli to garnish.

BLACK BEAN & CHILLI ENCHILADAS

Enchiladas are one of my go-to comfort foods. Rice and beans together in a convenient wrap, finished off with some melted cheese on top . . . They tick every box.

To make one portion

- ½ mug of basmati rice
- 1 mug of water for the rice, plus 25ml for the tortillas
- ½ red onion, sliced
- 1 tsp cumin seeds
- 100g black beans (from a 400g tin), drained
- ½ red chilli, sliced
- Small handful of chopped coriander
- 40g plain flour
- Splash of tomato passata
- Small handful of grated Cheddar cheese
- Olive oil
- Salt and pepper

To cook

Cook the rice in the water then remove from the heat and fluff with a fork.

Pan-fry the onion in a splash of olive oil over a medium heat for a few minutes before adding the cumin seeds, black beans and sliced chilli. Season with salt and pepper and continue to fry for a few more minutes. Remove from the heat and add the coriander.

Make the tortillas by mixing the flour with the 25ml of water and a pinch of salt in a bowl. Knead on a floured worktop until smooth, then cut into 2 balls. Using a rolling pin, roll each ball into a circle approximately 15cm in diameter. Heat a dry frying pan over a high heat, place the tortillas, one at a time, in the pan and cook for about 5 seconds on each side.

Preheat the grill to high. Spoon half the rice and half the beans down the centre of each tortilla, then roll up and place in an oven-proof dish. Top with a splash of tomato passata, add a pinch of salt and pepper and sprinkle over the grated Cheddar. Cook for about 7 minutes under the grill until the cheese is melted.

EVEN EASIER FALAFEL

Oven-roast the chickpeas for that falafel crunch, and chuck in the rest of the usual ingredients for that classic flavour.

To make one portion

100g chickpeas (from a 400g tin), drained

1 tsp ground cumin

Small handful of coriander, chopped

1 pitta bread, toasted

Salad (lettuce, onion and tomatoes)

Dollop of hummus

Olive oil

Salt and pepper

To cook

Preheat your oven to 180°C/gas mark 4.

Put the chickpeas in a baking tray, then drizzle with olive oil, season with salt and pepper, and sprinkle over the cumin. Roast for about 20 minutes until crispy, then remove from the oven and stir in the chopped coriander. Stuff into a toasted pitta bread with whatever salad you've got, plus a big dollop of hummus. Enjoy straight away.

PEANUT BUTTER CURRY

That's right: peanut butter isn't just for sandwiches. It's actually the key ingredient in some curries too. This recipe is a great way to use up the bits from an old jar.

To make one portion

- ½ mug basmati rice
- 1 mug water
- ½ aubergine, chopped into big chunks
- Splash of sesame oil
- 1 garlic clove, grated
- 2cm piece of fresh root ginger, grated

- 1 tsp curry powder
- 1 tbsp peanut butter
- 200g coconut milk (from a 400g tin)
- A few coriander leaves (optional)
- A few slices of red chilli (optional)
- Salt and pepper

To cook

Put the rice and the water in a saucepan with a pinch of salt. Cover with a lid and place over a medium heat for about 7 minutes until all the water is absorbed and the rice is cooked.

Meanwhile, fry the aubergine in a dry pan over a medium heat for about 8 minutes, then add the sesame oil, garlic, ginger, curry powder and peanut butter. Continue to cook for a few minutes more, then add the coconut milk and simmer for about 10 minutes until it's nice and thick. Season to taste, then serve with the rice, garnished with a few coriander leaves and chilli slices.

> **Tip** You can use up the rest of the coconut milk in another curry recipe – try the Thai Pea Curry on page 120.

THAI PEA CURRY

This is a quick and easy dinner, but it packs a healthy and tasty punch. You can add in any other veg you've got kicking around in the fridge, like carrots cut into matchsticks, diced peppers or a few broccoli florets.

To make one portion

½ mug of rice

1 mug of water

1 onion, sliced

A few small potatoes, halved

1 tbsp Thai green curry paste (see Tip)

200ml coconut milk (from a 400ml tin)

Handful of frozen peas

Handful of mangetout (optional)

1 red chilli, sliced, or a pinch of dried chilli flakes

Olive oil

Salt and pepper

To cook

Put the rice and the water in a saucepan with a lid and place over a medium heat. After about 7 minutes, when all the water is absorbed and the rice is cooked, turn off the heat and set aside.

Meanwhile, pan-fry the onion and potatoes in a splash of oil over a medium heat for about 10 minutes until they just start to colour. Add the Thai green curry paste and coconut milk and stir. Simmer for a few minutes, then add the peas and mangetout and simmer for a few minutes more until the vegetables are cooked. If the potatoes are taking a while and the sauce becomes too thick, just loosen with a splash of water. Season to taste, then garnish with sliced red chilli or dried chilli flakes and serve with the rice.

> Tip Some Thai curry pastes contain fish sauce, so remember to check the label if you're vegan or vegetarian.

SWEET POTATO KATSU CURRY

You could technically use any vegetable here, but I find that sweet potato works perfectly with the light and crispy tempura batter to make the perfect vegan curry.

To make one portion

½ mug of basmati rice

1 mug of water, plus 150ml cold water for the batter

100g self-raising flour

4 x 1cm-thick slices of sweet potato

1 tsp plain flour

1 tsp curry powder

5 tsp golden syrup

Soy sauce

1 spring onion, sliced lengthways

Vegetable oil

Salt

To cook

Put the rice and the mug of water in a saucepan with a pinch of salt, and cook over a medium heat with the lid on for about 7 minutes. When all the water has been absorbed and the rice is cooked, turn off the heat. Remove the lid and fluff up the rice.

Turn on the deep-fat fryer to pre-heat, or heat some vegetable oil (about 3cm deep) in a saucepan. Whisk the self-raising flour with the 150ml water and a pinch of salt in a bowl. Dip the slices of sweet potato into the batter then fry them in the oil for about 10 minutes until golden and crisp and cooked all the way through. Remove with a slotted spoon and drain on kitchen paper.

To make the sauce, put a frying pan over a medium heat and add the plain flour, curry powder and golden syrup. Stir to create a paste, then start adding water little by little to create a sauce (you will probably need about 200ml in total). Finish by adding a splash of soy sauce. Assemble the dish with the rice, sweet potato and sauce, then garnish with the spring onion.

PORTOBELLO KIEV

It's difficult to stuff a mushroom with garlic butter – trust me, I've tried. Then I came up with this: my mushroom Kiev. The breadcrumb coating gets nice and crispy, then you add the garlic butter as a sauce at the end. Genius!

To make one portion

1 portobello mushroom

Small handful of breadcrumbs (grated stale bread)

Small handful of chopped parsley, plus a pinch for the topping

1 large potato, peeled

3 garlic cloves

3 tbsp butter

Olive oil

Salt and pepper

To cook

Preheat your oven to 190°C/gas mark 5.

Rub the mushroom with olive oil. Mix the breadcrumbs in a bowl with a splash of olive oil, the pinch of chopped parsley, and some salt and pepper. Put the mushroom on a baking tray, top the mushroom with the breadcrumb and parsley mixture and cook in the oven for about 15 minutes, until the breadcrumbs are golden brown.

Meanwhile, cut the potato into rough chunks, add to a saucepan of salted boiling water and cook for about 15 minutes until tender, then drain, return to the pan, mash with a glug of olive oil and season with a pinch each of salt and pepper.

To make the sauce, pan-fry the garlic in a splash of olive oil over a medium heat for a few minutes until sizzling (but not browned), add the butter and fry for a few more minutes, adding the parsley just before the garlic starts to brown. Serve the sauce drizzled over the baked mushroom and mashed potato.

HOT TABBOULEH

Bulgur wheat is economical and delicious but in the UK it is really underused, so I've created a simple dish that you can make easily and which will hopefully give you the inspiration and confidence to use it more. Even better, you'll fall in love with this amazing ingredient.

To make one portion

Handful of bulgur wheat

2 spring onions, roughly chopped

½ red pepper, diced

Olive oil

Salt and pepper

To cook

Start by cooking the bulgur wheat in salted boiling water for about 12 minutes until soft, then drain.

Meanwhile, pan-fry the spring onions and pepper in a generous glug of olive oil and a pinch each of salt and pepper for about 5 minutes. Then add the bulgur wheat and mix everything together.

Season to taste, then serve.

GRIDDLED VEGETABLE COUSCOUS

This is a great recipe for when you have loads of leftover veg. Just chuck them on a hot griddle pan until they have char marks. The couscous bulks out a few vegetables to create a delicious plate of food, and the feta is a lovely, decadent topping.

To make one portion

A few long 5mm-thick slices of courgette

A few 5mm-thick slices of red pepper

A few 5mm-thick slices of red onion

Pinch of dried oregano

¼ vegetable stock cube

¼ mug of boiling water

¼ mug of couscous

Small handful of crumbled feta

Olive oil

Salt and pepper

To cook

Preheat your griddle pan (or a frying pan) over a medium-high heat.

Coat the vegetables in a splash of olive oil and sprinkle with a pinch each of salt and pepper and the oregano. Cook them on the hot pan for a couple of minutes on each side until nicely charred and tender.

Dissolve the stock cube in the boiling water, then add the stock to the mug of couscous. Let it rest for about 5 minutes, then fluff the couscous with a fork and mix with the griddled veg. Top with the crumbled feta and serve.

> **Make it vegan** Leave out the feta to make this dish vegan friendly.

ONE-POT
PLEASERS

ROASTED ALOO GOBI

Roasted veg is the best, not least because you can cook it all in one tray! Here, I've just infused the veg with some lovely curry flavours to make one of my favourite One Pound Meals. Roasted Aloo Gobi is a great example of how oven-baking can freshen up a typically greasy dish.

To make one portion

¼ cauliflower, cut into small florets

1 potato, cubed

2 tsp curry powder

Handful of frozen peas

Handful of spinach

Olive oil

Salt and pepper

To cook

Preheat your oven to 190°C/gas mark 5.

Throw the cauliflower florets into an ovenproof dish along with the cubed potato. Drizzle with olive oil and sprinkle over the curry powder. Mix everything together and roast in the oven for 40 minutes.

After the vegetables have been roasting for 40 minutes, add the frozen peas, stir them in and roast for a further 5 minutes or until they are cooked. Remove the dish from the oven and stir in the spinach, using the heat of the roasted veg to wilt it.

Season with salt and pepper, then serve in a bowl.

COCONUT CHICKPEA CURRY

A super simple curry using tinned chickpeas and coconut milk. If you're ever stuck for time, dig a couple of cans out of the kitchen cupboard and give this a go.

To make one portion

- ½ onion, diced
- 1 garlic clove, grated
- 1 thumb-sized piece of ginger, grated
- 1 tsp curry powder
- 1 red chilli, chopped
- 200g chickpeas (from a 400g tin), drained
- 200g coconut milk (from a 400g tin)
- Small handful of chopped coriander, to serve
- Olive oil
- Salt and pepper

To cook

Start by pan-frying the onion in a splash of oil over a medium heat for a few minutes. Add the garlic, ginger, curry powder and half the chilli, then continue to fry for a few more minutes. Next add the chickpeas and fry for a further couple of minutes before adding the coconut milk and simmering for 5 minutes. Season to taste and serve garnished with coriander and the rest of the chilli.

> **Tip** This dish is easy to scale up, so you can make a bigger batch and freeze the leftovers for another time

GREEN BEAN & LENTIL CURRY

Lentils are a delicious way to bulk out a meal, and they take on other flavours really well. This fantastic lentil-based curry uses pre-cooked lentils, which means it takes no time at all to make.

To make one portion

½ onion, sliced

1 garlic clove, sliced

Small handful of green beans

1 tsp curry powder

200g green lentils (from a 400g tin), drained

½ vegetable stock cube

Splash of cream

Olive oil

Salt and pepper

To cook

Pan-fry the sliced onion, garlic and green beans in a splash of olive oil over a medium heat for a few minutes until the garlic starts to brown, then add the curry powder and the lentils. Fry for another minute, then add a big splash of water, crumble in the stock cube and simmer for a few minutes until the beans are cooked and the sauce thickens.

Season to taste with salt and pepper and serve with a splash of cream.

> **Make it vegan** To make this dish vegan, swap the splash of cream for a plant-based cream.

BEETROOT CURRY

Ever wondered what else you can make with beetroot? This is my super-easy Beetroot Curry, made lighter and healthier by using crème fraîche. Ready in minutes, it's packed with all the flavour and goodness of beetroot.

To make one portion

½ red onion, cut into wedges

1 pre-cooked beetroot, cut into wedges

1 tsp curry powder

2 tbsp crème fraîche

Pinch of dried chilli flakes

Olive oil

Salt and pepper

To cook

Pan-fry the onion and beetroot in a splash of olive oil over a medium heat. After about 5 minutes, once the onion has softened, stir in the curry powder and make sure everything is evenly coated. Cook for 1 minute, then add the crème fraîche, salt and pepper and simmer for a couple more minutes.

Serve in a bowl garnished with the chilli flakes.

COCONUT DAAL

By using coconut milk, you can create a luxurious and creamy daal that is totally vegan. This is a lovely, comforting dish of food.

To make one portion

½ onion, sliced

1 garlic clove, sliced

Handful of red lentils

1 tsp curry powder

200g coconut milk (from 400g tin)

1 mug of water

200g chickpeas (from 400g tin), drained

Small handful of spinach

Olive oil

Salt and pepper

To cook

Grab a saucepan and fry the onion and garlic in a splash of olive oil over a medium heat for about 5 minutes until soft and cooked. Add the lentils and curry powder and stir, coating the lentils in the oil. Next add the coconut milk and the water and simmer for about 15 minutes until the lentils are cooked (adding more water if needed). About 5 minutes before the end of the cooking time, add the chickpeas and season to taste. Just before serving add the spinach, stirring it through so it wilts.

JOLLOF RICE

This is a rich and spicy rice dish with stewed onions, garlic, tomatoes and plenty of dried chilli flakes, but with the cooling addition of sliced banana at the end.

To make one portion

1 tbsp tomato purée

½ onion, roughly diced

1 garlic clove, sliced

½ red pepper, roughly diced

Generous pinch of chilli flakes

200g chopped tomatoes (from a 400g tin)

½ mug of rice

1 mug of water

½ vegetable stock cube

½ banana, sliced

Olive oil

Salt and pepper

To cook

Start by grabbing a high-sided pan and pan-frying the tomato purée, onion, garlic and red pepper in a splash of oil over a medium heat for about 5 minutes. Then add the chilli flakes, chopped tomatoes, rice, water and stock cube. Season and simmer for about 10 minutes until the rice is cooked (adding more water if required). Finally, add the chopped banana, season to taste and serve.

BANG BANG CAULIFLOWER

My Bang Bang Cauliflower has all the familiar Chinese-style sweet and spicy flavours but is a delicious and healthy alternative to those expensive takeaways.

To make one portion

Handful of cauliflower florets

1 garlic clove, sliced

Pinch of dried chilli flakes

Sesame oil

100g passata (from a 400g tin)

2 tbsp honey

Pinch of sesame seeds

½ spring onion, sliced

Salt and pepper

To cook

Grab a saucepan, throw in the cauliflower florets, garlic and chilli flakes, season with salt and pepper, then fry in a splash of sesame oil over a medium heat. Just before the garlic starts to brown, add the passata and honey. Simmer for 5–10 minutes until the liquid reduces and sticks to the cauliflower, adding a tiny splash of water if the sauce gets too thick. Once the cauliflower is soft, remove the pan from the heat and serve it with a sprinkle of sesame seeds, a drizzle of sesame oil and a garnish of sliced spring onion.

THAI-STYLE RED CURRY NOODLES

Sriracha is a huge shortcut ingredient when you crave spicy food. There's no need for chillies and endless spices: just add a squirt of sriracha and you are minutes away from a simple £1 Thai-inspired curry.

To make one portion

½ red onion, sliced

1 garlic clove, sliced

Splash of sesame oil

100ml coconut milk (from a 400ml tin)

100ml water

Big squirt of sriracha

Small handful of udon noodles (pre-cooked, from a pouch)

A few broccoli stalks

Pinch of sesame seeds

Soy sauce

To cook

Pan-fry the onion and garlic in the sesame oil over a medium heat for a few minutes until the garlic starts to brown. Add the coconut milk, water and sriracha. Simmer for a minute, then add the noodles and broccoli. Continue to simmer for about 5 minutes until the broccoli is cooked.

Transfer to a bowl, sprinkle with the sesame seeds and add a splash of soy sauce.

THAI DAUPHINOISE

Coconut milk plays such an important part in Thai cooking and is a great vegan substitute for cream. This gave me an idea! I used coconut milk to make a Thai version of a classic French dauphinoise.

To make one portion

Handful of baby potatoes, sliced

Sesame oil

100ml coconut milk (from a 400g tin)

1 garlic clove, crushed

Pinch of dried chilli flakes (or dried chillies)

½ pak choi, sliced lengthways

Splash of soy sauce

Salt and pepper

To cook

Preheat your oven to 190°C/gas mark 5.

Arrange the potatoes in an ovenproof dish, drizzle with sesame oil, season with salt and pepper, then bake in the oven for 10 minutes.

After 10 minutes, add the coconut milk to the potatoes, along with crushed garlic and chilli flakes, and top with the pak choi. Drizzle with sesame oil and bake for another 10 minutes.

Remove from the oven and serve with a splash of soy sauce.

CUMIN-SPICED LENTILS & POTATOES WITH SPINACH & YOGURT

Quick and easy, this makes a great lunchtime treat and is a fantastic way to use up any leftover potatoes without the hassle of having to boil them first: just chop them up small and cook it all in the same pan.

To make one portion

- 1 potato, diced, skin on
- ½ onion, sliced
- ½ tsp ground cumin
- 3 handfuls frozen spinach, defrosted
- 200g green lentils (from a 400g tin), drained
- 2 dollops of natural yogurt
- Olive oil
- Salt and pepper

To cook

Pan-fry the diced potato in a splash of olive oil over a medium heat for about 10 minutes until almost cooked, then add the onion and cumin and fry for a further 5 minutes. Next add the spinach. Season to taste, then add the lentils and a big dollop of yogurt. Cook for a few minutes more, then serve, garnished with another dollop of yogurt.

> **Swap** For a vegan version, swap the natural yogurt for coconut yogurt.

PULLED PORK CHILLI

If you substitute minced beef for homemade pulled pork, you'll get the best chilli ever. And by slow-cooking the chilli, the flavour gets to develop for much longer; you'll certainly notice the difference. Don't be tempted to leave out the crème fraîche – it plays an important part in balancing the flavours as it gives a fresh zing to a very earthy and hearty dish.

To make one portion

- 2 pork belly slices (approx. 150g total weight)
- 1 red onion, thickly sliced
- 1 garlic clove, sliced
- 1 tsp ground cumin
- 1 tsp paprika
- 1 tsp plain flour
- 200g chopped tomatoes (from a 400g tin)
- 1 beef stock cube
- 150ml water
- 200g kidney beans (from a 400g tin, drained)
- 1 tbsp crème fraîche
- A few thin slices of spring onion tips
- Olive oil
- Salt and pepper

To cook

Start by seasoning and frying the pork belly slices in a saucepan with a splash of oil. When they are nicely browned, add the onion and then a few minutes later the garlic. As the garlic just starts to brown, add the cumin, paprika and flour. Stir until all the flour disappears, then add the chopped tomatoes, crumble in the stock cube and add the water.

Simmer gently over a low heat for 1½ hours with the lid on then, 10 minutes before serving, add the kidney beans and simmer with the lid off. If you find there's not enough liquid in the pan, add a splash more water.

Using two forks, tear the pork apart into chunks, then serve the chilli with a big dollop of crème fraîche and sliced spring onion tips.

CHICKEN DRUMSTICK CASSOULET

One of my favourite complete meals in a pot has to be cassoulet: you get the carb element from the beans, a lovely rich sauce and whatever you choose as the hero ingredient. Here I have gone for chicken drumsticks, which are affordable and delicious.

To make one portion

- 2 chicken drumsticks, skin on
- ½ red onion, sliced
- 200g cannellini beans (from a 400g tin), drained
- Pinch of dried oregano
- 200g chopped tomatoes (from a 400g tin)
- ½ vegetable stock cube
- Olive oil
- Salt and pepper

To cook

Season the chicken drumsticks with salt and pepper, then pan-fry in a splash of olive oil over a medium heat for about 10 minutes, turning occasionally to colour all sides.

Add the onion and continue to fry for a further 5 minutes. Add the cannellini beans, oregano and chopped tomatoes, then crumble in the stock cube and season. Simmer for about 10 minutes, then serve.

> **Swap** If you don't have cannellini beans, swap them for canned chickpeas.

CANNELLINI BEANS WITH LEEK & TOMATOES

This simple, humble bean stew is perfect for eating on a budget. The splash of red wine vinegar gives it a great little kick. If you're not confident with balancing flavours with vinegar, then this is the dish to get you started: just give it a taste before and after and you'll see the difference it makes.

To make one portion

¼ leek, roughly chopped

1 garlic clove, sliced

Handful of cherry tomatoes

200g cannellini beans (from a 400g tin), drained

Pinch of dried oregano

½ vegetable stock cube

Small splash of red wine vinegar

Olive oil

Salt and pepper

To cook

Pan-fry the leek, garlic and tomatoes in a generous glug of olive oil over a medium heat, with a pinch each of salt and pepper, for about 5 minutes. When the garlic starts to brown, add the beans and oregano, and crumble in the stock cube. Fry for another couple of minutes, then add the splash of red wine vinegar and a splash of water. Simmer for a few minutes, then serve, drizzled with a generous glug of olive oil.

BACON & WHITE BEAN NO-BLEND SOUP

When I'm at home I try to avoid getting the blender out as it just creates more washing up. This no-blend recipe means I can enjoy a warming, hearty bowl of soup without any of the hassle.

To make one portion

¼ onion, sliced

1 garlic clove, sliced

3 rashers of smoked streaky bacon, chopped

200g cannellini beans (from a 400g tin)

½ chicken stock cube

Small handful of spinach

Olive oil

Salt and pepper

To cook

Gently fry the onion in a saucepan with a splash of olive oil over a medium heat. Once it has softened, add the garlic and bacon, then continue to fry for a few minutes. Add the cannellini beans just before the garlic and bacon start to colour, along with half of the liquid from the tin and a splash more water. Crumble in the stock cube and simmer for about 5 minutes until the soup is the required thickness. Season to taste with salt and pepper and add the spinach leaves. Once the leaves have wilted, the soup is ready to serve.

LEFTOVER BREAD PANZANELLA

This dish is perfect for using up leftover bread – in fact, you need it to be a little stale, or it will go too soggy. It's a tasty and satisfying summer dish.

To make one portion

A few slices of stale sourdough bread, torn into chunks

A few tomatoes, roughly chopped (any tomatoes will do)

1 red onion, sliced

1 tbsp balsamic vinegar

A few basil leaves, to garnish (optional)

Olive oil

Salt and pepper

To cook

Place the chunks of stale bread in a bowl, along with the tomatoes and red onion. Add a generous pinch of salt and pepper, along with the balsamic vinegar and 5 tbsp olive oil. Mix it all together, then leave to stand for 5 minutes. Now give it another mix, garnish with a few basil leaves and serve.

> **Tip** I have to admit, sometimes I buy new bread just to make this recipe. If you decide to do the same, you just need to dry it out in the oven for a bit first.

HASSELBACK SQUASH

Hasselback potatoes are a fun and exciting way to cook potatoes if you are bored of the usual chips, wedges and mash. So, I took this style of preparation and made it into a main meal by creating a hasselback butternut squash. If you wanted to make this into a vegetarian recipe, then you can simply leave out the Parma ham.

To make one portion

- ½ butternut squash, seeds scraped out
- 2 slices of Parma ham, each halved
- 20g feta cheese, crumbled
- 1 tsp dried oregano
- Olive oil
- Salt and pepper

To cook

Preheat your oven to 190°C/gas mark 5.

Cut four v-shaped slits into the squash, making sure you don't cut all the way through.

Fold the pieces of Parma ham in half and lay one in each slit, then fill with a combination of crumbled feta and oregano, pressing it into the slits using your fingers.

Drizzle with olive oil, season with salt and pepper, then bake in the oven on a baking tray for about 30 minutes, until the squash is cooked all the way through.

SAUSAGE & POLENTA BAKE

I knew there had to be a simple way of cooking polenta, so I devised this huge shortcut to create a tasty oven-baked polenta dish that requires just 2 minutes prep and no stirring or checking while it's cooking.

To make one portion

1 egg-cup of polenta

4 egg-cups of milk

1 sausage

A few cherry tomatoes (on the vine)

Olive oil

Salt and pepper

To cook

Preheat your oven to 190°C/gas mark 5.

Put the polenta and milk in an ovenproof dish or pan. Season with salt and pepper, stir, then throw in the sausage and the tomatoes.

Bake in the oven for about 35 minutes until the sausage is nicely browned, then serve garnished with cracked black pepper and a glug of olive oil.

HALLOUMI, AUBERGINE & TOMATO BAKE

Easy dinners are my speciality, making them look tasty with minimum effort. Halloumi goes a lovely golden brown in the oven and looks stunning here layered between slices of roasted aubergine. It's much easier than it looks. I've suggested you go for 4 servings here, as the dish makes a great centrepiece.

To make 4 portions

- 2 onions, sliced
- 4 garlic cloves, crushed or grated
- 400g tin chopped tomatoes
- 1 tsp dried oregano, plus an extra pinch
- 2 aubergines, sliced into 1cm thick slices
- 2 x 200g blocks of halloumi, sliced into 1cm thick slices
- Olive oil
- Salt and pepper

To cook

Preheat your oven to 180°C/gas mark 4.

Grab a casserole dish and use it to fry the onions in a splash of oil over a medium heat for about 5 minutes until nice and soft, adding the crushed garlic for the final minute. Add the chopped tomatoes and the 1 tsp oregano. Simmer for a few minutes and season to taste.

Arrange slices of aubergine and halloumi on top, alternating between the two, then drizzle with olive oil and sprinkle with an extra pinch of oregano. Bake in the oven for about 25 minutes until slightly browned on top, then serve.

> **Swap** Courgettes and freshly sliced tomatoes also work brilliantly in this dish, so use what you have available.

CHICKEN & PEPPER TRAYBAKE

Oven-roasted peppers have a rich, sticky texture that perfectly complements the roasted chicken in this easy traybake recipe. If you like, you can add some chorizo, for an extra punch of flavour.

To make one portion

1 chicken thigh, skin on

Pinch of paprika

1 red pepper, roughly chopped or torn into big chunks

A few slices of cooking chorizo (optional)

Olive oil

To cook

Preheat your oven to 180°C/gas mark 4.

Rub the chicken with olive oil, salt, black pepper and paprika. Place on a baking tray and roast for about 30 minutes, adding the pepper and chorizo (if using) halfway through.

Serve drizzled with all those lovely paprika-infused juices left in the tray.

ONE-POT FETA & CHERRY TOMATO ORZO

I wanted to make an even easier version of that pasta dish that went viral on TikTok, so instead of cooking the pasta separately, I just used orzo and threw it in the same dish.

To make one portion

100g feta cheese

Handful of cherry tomatoes

Handful of orzo

Pinch of dried oregano

75ml water

Fresh basil leaves, to serve (optional)

Olive oil

Salt and pepper

To cook

Preheat your oven to 180°C/gas mark 4.

Put the feta, tomatoes and orzo in an ovenproof dish. Sprinkle over the oregano and season with salt and pepper, then add a couple of big glugs of olive oil and the water. Cook in the oven for about 20 minutes, checking halfway through to see if you need a splash more water. Give the orzo a quick stir at this point, but don't break up the tomatoes and feta too much.

Once it's cooked through, remove from the oven and give it another little stir to break up the feta and tomatoes. Scatter over some fresh basil leaves (if using), then serve.

MUSHROOM ORZO

Orzo pasta is such a versatile ingredient and features more and more in my everyday cooking. It's easy to cook and allows you to take huge shortcuts to create speedy one-pan meals – like this mushroom dish – at a moment's notice.

To make one portion

Handful of mushrooms, sliced

Pinch of dried oregano

Handful of dried orzo

75ml water

½ vegetable stock cube

Olive oil

Salt and pepper

To cook

Season the mushrooms and pan-fry them in a splash of olive oil with the oregano over a medium heat for about 5 minutes. Then, add a splash more oil and the orzo, letting the orzo absorb some of the oil. Add the water, crumble in the stock cube and let the orzo simmer. After about 5 minutes, once the orzo has absorbed most of the water, check to see if it is cooked (add some more water if needed and continue cooking if it's not ready).

Once the orzo is cooked, remove the pan from the heat, drizzle the dish with a glug of olive oil, sprinkle with some cracked black pepper and serve.

CABBAGE RIBBON STIR-FRY

Sneak some extra greens into your meal with this simple and healthy swap from noodles to cabbage. Just cut it into strips and it'll do a similar job – and you don't need to boil the ribbons first, so that's some washing-up saved, too. Here I've used one of my favourite dipping sauces as a sauce for the ribbons.

To make one portion

⅛ white cabbage, cut into strips

½ red onion, cut into wedges

1 carrot, cut into matchsticks

1 spring onion, roughly chopped

1 garlic clove, sliced

1 tbsp Chinese crispy chilli sauce in oil, plus 1 tsp to garnish

Sesame oil

Salt and pepper

To cook

Season the cabbage strips with salt and pepper, then pan-fry in a splash of sesame oil and a splash of water over a medium heat for a few minutes until softened. Add the red onion, carrot, spring onion and garlic, and continue to pan-fry for a few more minutes. Stir in the crispy chilli sauce, then serve with extra sauce to garnish.

REVISION
MIND
FEEDERS

FISHERMAN'S MACARONI PIE

This is a wholesome hunger-busting dish. By using a breadcrumb topping instead of mashed potato, adding uncooked macaroni, frozen fish and frozen peas, I've created a simple and easy recipe that you'll cook over and over again.

To make one portion

1 tbsp butter

1 tsp plain flour

300ml milk

Handful of macaroni

1 frozen white fish fillet

Handful of frozen peas

Stale bread, torn into small chunks

Olive oil

Salt and pepper

To cook

Grab an ovenproof pan*, add the butter and melt it over a medium heat. Stir in the flour to create a paste and cook for a further minute. Gradually add the milk, stirring continuously, and cook until you have a smooth sauce. Throw in the macaroni and simmer for a few minutes then add the frozen fish. Cook for about 10 minutes until the fish has defrosted and is cooked and flaky, season with salt and pepper, add the frozen peas and continue to cook for 2 more minutes.

Remove from the heat and sprinkle the bread chunks over the filling, along with a pinch of salt, some cracked black pepper and a generous glug of olive oil.

Finish the pie under a hot grill for a few minutes until the breadcrumbs are nice and golden brown.

* If you don't have a pan with an ovenproof handle, then just use your normal pan and transfer the filling to an ovenproof dish before adding the breadcrumb top.

PESCE AL FORNO

By oven-roasting a few simple ingredients with just olive oil and loads of pepper, you can create a wonderfully rich and intense sauce. As the tinned tomatoes and garlic slowly bubble away in this fish dish, their flavours magnify, while the fish slowly cooks on top. This is an easy, no mess, one-dish recipe that takes minutes to prep and throw in the oven.

To make one portion

200g chopped tomatoes (from a 400g tin)

1 garlic clove, crushed

A few black pitted olives

½ tsp dried oregano

1 frozen white fish fillet

Olive oil

Salt and pepper

To cook

Preheat your oven to 190°C/gas mark 5.

Grab a small ovenproof dish and tip in the chopped tomatoes, then add the garlic, olives and season with the oregano and some salt and pepper.

Place the frozen fish fillet on top and drizzle with a very generous glug of olive oil, sprinkling the fish with a pinch of salt and loads of cracked black pepper.

Cook in the oven for about 30 minutes, until the fish is cooked and starts to flake, then remove from the oven and serve.

HOT SALAD NIÇOISE

Here I have updated one of the most famous salads of all time to create a warm smoked version with a zingy mustard dressing and a gooey soft-boiled egg. This recipe uses just one saucepan of boiling water to cook the three hot elements of the dish, saving you time and washing up.

To make one portion

1 egg

Handful of green beans

A few cherry vine tomatoes (on the vine)

1 tsp Dijon mustard

1 smoked mackerel fillet, flaked

A couple of slices of red onion

Olive oil

Salt and pepper

To cook

Bring a pan of salted water to the boil, add the egg and cook for 7½ minutes. Once boiled, use a spoon to take the egg out of the water then stop the egg cooking any further by cooling it under cold running water. Add the green beans and tomatoes to the boiling water and remove after a few minutes, once the beans are cooked and tender and the tomatoes have softened.

Meanwhile, mix the Dijon mustard with 2 teaspoons of olive oil to create a dressing.

Peel the boiled egg, cut it in half and serve it with the beans, tomatoes, flaked smoked mackerel and onion. Finish the dish with a drizzle of the Dijon dressing and a pinch of salt and pepper.

FISH EN PAPILLOTE

This is what frozen fish was made for: hassle-free and delicious meals at a moment's notice. Here, I have used an old technique of cooking ingredients in greaseproof paper – it locks in the moisture and steams the fish, potatoes and fennel, leaving you with more free time and no washing up.

To make one portion

A few small potatoes, thinly sliced

½ fennel bulb, thinly sliced

1 frozen white fish fillet

Wedge of lemon (optional)

Olive oil

Salt and pepper

To cook

Preheat your oven to 190°C/gas mark 5.

Grab a square sheet of greaseproof paper and lay some sliced potatoes in the middle, season with salt and pepper, then add a layer of sliced fennel and place the frozen fish fillet on top. Add a glug of olive oil and season with a pinch of salt and plenty of cracked black pepper.

Wrap the paper around the fish and fold it tightly to make a parcel, then place it in the oven on a baking tray for about 40 minutes, until the fish is cooked through.

Unwrap the parcel and enjoy your meal straight from the paper, with a wedge of lemon if you like.

WHITE BEAN FISH CASSOULET

You won't believe that with just two minutes prep and an awkwardly balanced frozen fillet, you'll be sitting down to eat this amazing recipe.

To make one portion

¼ leek, rinsed and cut into roughly 7mm-thick circles

200g cannellini beans (from a 400g tin)

1 garlic clove, crushed

20ml milk

1 frozen white fish fillet

Olive oil

Salt and pepper

To cook

Preheat your oven to 190°C/gas mark 5.

Throw the leek circles into an ovenproof dish, along with the cannellini beans, garlic and milk.

Season well with salt and pepper, give it a quick stir and place the frozen fish fillet on top, straight from the freezer. Drizzle everything with a big glug of olive oil and don't forget to season the fish with salt and loads of cracked black pepper (the oil will help it stick to the fish).

Bake for about 25 minutes, until the fish is cooked through.

MACKEREL FISH CAKES & PARSLEY SAUCE

This is a great recipe – you'll love dipping the smoky, crispy fish cakes into the light, refreshing lemon and parsley sauce.

To make one portion

1 smoked mackerel fillet, flaked	125ml milk
2 tbsp breadcrumbs (grated stale bread)	1 tsp dried (or chopped fresh) parsley
1 spring onion, finely chopped	Squeeze of lemon juice
1 egg, beaten	Olive oil
2 tsp plain flour	Salt and pepper

To cook

Mix the flaked mackerel, breadcrumbs, spring onion, egg and 1 teaspoon of the flour together in a bowl to form the fish cake mixture. Season well with salt and pepper.

Heat a splash of olive oil in a pan over a medium heat and spoon the fish cake mixture into the pan in three dollops. Turn the fish cakes over after about 5 minutes, then fry for a further 5 minutes, until the middle is cooked through and the outside is golden brown.

Meanwhile, to make the sauce, add a tiny splash of olive oil to a pan over a medium heat and add the rest of the flour. Stir with a whisk and slowly add the milk to create a creamy sauce. When the sauce has thickened, season with salt and pepper and add the parsley and lemon juice.

Place the fish cakes in the middle of the lemon and parsley sauce.

SMOKED MACKEREL PATÉ

This is something I make all the time. I love the smoky flavour of the mackerel and the way it balances so perfectly with the crème fraîche. This is a sophisticated tuna mayo for hipsters, so make sure you have char lines on your toasted sourdough bread!

To make one portion

1 smoked mackerel fillet, flaked

1 tbsp crème fraîche

2 slices of sourdough bread

Small handful of rocket

Olive oil

Salt and pepper

To cook

Mix the mackerel and the crème fraîche together in a bowl, then season with a tiny bit of salt and loads of pepper.

Heat a dry griddle pan over a high heat. Drizzle both sides of the bread slices with olive oil, add a sprinkle of salt then griddle on each side, until toasted, with char marks.

To serve, spread the mackerel paté on the toast thickly and garnish with a few rocket leaves and more black pepper.

SMOKY FISH TACOS

Using smoked mackerel gives these fish tacos an extra smoky flavour with zero extra effort! Just throw the ingredients in the pan
(the mackerel is already cooked so making the filling takes just
minutes), then knock up a few tortillas.

To make one portion

¼ red onion, roughly diced

200g chopped tomatoes (from
  a 400g tin)

1 smoked mackerel fillet, flaked

1 tsp ground cumin

1 tsp paprika

40g plain flour, plus extra for
  dusting

25ml cold water

3 tsp crème fraîche

1 spring onion, sliced

1 lemon wedge, to serve
  (optional)

Olive oil

Salt and pepper

To cook

Pan-fry the onion in a splash of olive oil over a medium heat. As
soon as the onion starts to soften, throw in the chopped tomatoes, flaked mackerel, cumin and paprika. Season well with salt
and pepper and simmer for about 10 minutes to reduce the sauce.

Meanwhile, combine the flour, water and a pinch of salt in a bowl
to form a dough. Dust the worktop with a little flour, then knead
the dough on the worktop for a few minutes until smooth. Divide
the dough into three balls and roll each piece into a roughly 10cm
circle. Heat a dry frying pan over a high heat, add the flatbreads
and cook for about 2 minutes on each side until lightly toasted.

Now, assemble the tacos (while the flatbreads are still warm).
Spoon a little of the mackerel and tomato mixture onto each
taco, add a teaspoon of crème fraîche on top and garnish with
the sliced spring onion to add a bit of extra crunch. Serve with a
lemon wedge, if you like.

SARDINE PASTA

Tinned sardines have all the flavour of the sea, and are ideal for a quick hassle-free pasta sauce. Chuck in a few salty olives and the whole dish comes together in minutes to create this Mediterranean classic.

To make one portion

125g dried spaghetti

¼ red onion, roughly diced

1 garlic clove, sliced

200g chopped tomatoes (from a 400g tin)

120g tin of whole sardines in oil, drained

A few black pitted olives

Olive oil

Salt and pepper

To cook

Bring a pan of salted water to the boil and cook the spaghetti until al dente.

Meanwhile, pan-fry the onion in a splash of olive oil over a medium heat for a few minutes. Add the garlic and, just before it starts to brown, add the chopped tomatoes and season well with salt and pepper. Next, add the sardines and black olives then simmer for 5 minutes to reduce the sauce.

Serve the sauce on a bed of the spaghetti, drizzle with a generous glug of olive oil and add an extra sprinkling of cracked black pepper.

FARMHOUSE TOFU RICE

This quick and easy savoury rice dish is a warm and comforting recipe that highlights just how versatile tofu can be.

To make one portion

½ mug of brown rice

1 mug of water

½ vegetable stock cube

½ red onion, roughly diced

100g firm tofu, cubed

½ carrot, roughly diced

Small handful of pine nuts

Small handful of kale, roughly chopped

Olive oil

Salt and pepper

To cook

Put the rice and water in a saucepan, crumble in the stock cube and cook over a medium heat with the lid on for about 10 minutes, until all the water has been absorbed and the rice is cooked. Turn off the heat, remove the lid and fluff up the rice with a fork.

Meanwhile, pan-fry the onion in a splash of olive oil over a medium heat for a few minutes until softened, then add the tofu, carrot and pine nuts, season with salt and fry for a few more minutes.

Next, add the kale, plenty of cracked black pepper, a splash more olive oil and fry for about 5 more minutes until cooked and the kale is slightly charred on the edges.

Mix the tofu and carrot mixture with the cooked rice and serve.

TERIYAKI TOFU

Tofu is a green and sustainable substitute for meat. Here is an idea for a teriyaki-style dish using minimal ingredients.

To make one portion

½ mug of basmati rice

1 mug of water

A few pieces of tofu, cut into triangles

1 tbsp honey

1 garlic clove, crushed

Pinch of dried chilli flakes

1 tbsp soy sauce

Pinch of sesame seeds

1 spring onion, thinly sliced

To cook

Put the rice and the water in a saucepan with a pinch of salt. Cover with a lid and place over a medium heat for about 7 minutes until all the water is absorbed and the rice is cooked.

Season the tofu triangles with salt and pepper, then pan-fry in a splash of sesame oil over a medium heat for a few minutes on each side. Add the honey, garlic, chilli flakes and soy sauce to the pan, along with an extra splash of sesame oil. Bring to a simmer and use the sauce this creates to baste the tofu. After a few minutes, once the tofu is a nice dark brown, remove from the pan. Sprinkle over the sesame seeds and spring onion, and serve with the rice.

Swap For a vegan version, swap the honey for maple syrup.

MUSHROOM STROGANOFF

Here's a super-speedy vegan mushroom stroganoff for you to try. All the classic flavours are there, such as garlic and paprika, but in this dish the creaminess comes from a combination of oat milk and flour.

To make one portion

½ mug of brown rice

1 mug of water

1 portobello mushroom, cut into 1cm-thick slices

1 garlic clove, sliced

½ tsp paprika

1 tsp plain flour

150ml oat milk (or any milk substitute)

Small handful of spinach

Olive oil

Salt and pepper

To cook

Put the rice and water in a saucepan and cook over a medium heat with the lid on for about 15 minutes, until all the water has been absorbed and the rice is cooked.

Meanwhile, pan-fry the sliced mushroom in a splash of olive oil over a medium heat for a few minutes. When the mushroom is almost cooked, season with salt and pepper and add the garlic, along with a splash more olive oil and continue to fry until the garlic starts to brown. Add the paprika and flour to the pan and stir for another minute, then gradually pour in the milk, stirring constantly. Simmer for a few minutes until the sauce thickens. Add the spinach and allow it to wilt, then remove from the heat. Season to taste and serve with the rice.

LEEK & MUSHROOM POT PIE

A creamy leek sauce with mushrooms and a crispy pastry lid . . . this is food that gives you a nice warm hug on a cold day.

To make one portion

- 1 leek, sliced
- A few mushrooms, sliced
- 1 tsp plain flour
- 1 tsp Dijon mustard
- 200ml milk

- 10cm diameter circle of puff pastry
- 1 egg, beaten
- Olive oil
- Salt and pepper

To cook

Preheat your oven to 190°C/gas mark 5.

Season and pan-fry the leeks and mushrooms in a splash of olive oil over a medium heat for about 10 minutes until cooked. Then add the flour and mustard and continue cooking for a minute, stirring constantly, before slowly adding the milk, stirring all the time, to create a sauce. Simmer for a few more minutes to thicken a little, then transfer to a round ovenproof dish about 10cm in diameter.

Place the pastry lid on top of the filling, brush with the beaten egg and cook in the oven for about 30 minutes until golden brown.

> **Make it vegan** Use plant-based milk, vegan pastry and don't brush with egg.

LEEK & MUSHROOM BARLEY RISOTTO

Leeks and mushrooms are a robust flavour combination that you can always count on: nothing can go wrong when you're combining these two. It's guaranteed to be delicious.

To make one portion

½ onion, diced

Handful of pearl barley

½ vegetable stock cube

300ml water

½ leek, sliced

Handful of mushrooms, sliced

1 thyme sprig

Small handful of grated Parmesan cheese, plus a few shavings for garnish

Olive oil

Salt and pepper

To cook

Pan-fry the onion in a splash of olive oil over a medium heat for about 10 minutes until soft, then add the barley and cook for a further minute. Crumble in the ½ stock cube and pour over the water. Simmer for about 15–20 minutes until the barley is cooked but still retains a slight bite, adding more water if needed.

Meanwhile, pan-fry the leek and mushrooms in a splash of olive oil over a medium heat for about 12 minutes until soft, adding the thyme halfway through.

Stir some grated Parmesan into the barley risotto, then add the leek and mushrooms. Season to taste, and serve with a few shavings of Parmesan to garnish.

> **Swap** To make this vegetarian/vegan, omit the Parmesan cheese. If you like, you can replace it with a sprinkling of nutritional yeast.

COURGETTE & WHITE BEAN LASAGNE

My challenge here was to create a vegan white sauce that would form the perfect golden brown lasagne top – I discovered that a white-bean-based sauce did the trick.

To make one portion

- 1 onion, sliced
- 2 garlic cloves, sliced
- 200g cannellini beans (from a 400g tin), plus
- ½ the liquid from the tin
- 2 pinches of dried oregano
- 1 tsp plain flour

- ½ courgette, diced
- 200g chopped tomatoes (from a 400g tin)
- 2 dried lasagne sheets
- Small handful of grated butternut squash
- Olive oil
- Salt and pepper

To cook

To make the white sauce, pan-fry half the onion in a splash of olive oil over a medium heat for a few minutes until softened, then add half the sliced garlic and fry for a further minute. Add the cannellini beans and half the liquid from the tin. Sprinkle in a pinch of oregano, season and simmer for a few minutes until most of the water has evaporated and the beans are a bit mushy. Blitz in a blender with the flour until the mixture forms a paste and set to one side.

Pan-fry the remaining onion in a splash of olive oil over a medium heat for a few minutes until softened, then add the remaining sliced garlic and the courgette. Fry for a few more minutes, then add the chopped tomatoes. Add the remaining oregano, season with salt and pepper and simmer for about 5 minutes.

Pour half the tomato and courgette ragu into a small ovenproof dish, place a dried lasagne sheet on top, then spread over half the white sauce. Repeat the layers and top with the grated butternut squash. Bake in the oven for about 30 minutes until the top is golden brown, then serve.

POTATOES, ASPARAGUS & PEAS WITH GARLIC BUTTER

I know it's just potatoes and veg, but this tastes way more exciting than it sounds. Keep the potato skins on: they are nutritious and add a rustic wholesomeness to this simple dish.

To make one portion

Handful of baby potatoes

2 tbsp butter

2 garlic cloves, crushed

A few asparagus spears

A small handful of frozen peas, defrosted

Small handful of chopped parsley

Handful of grated Parmesan cheese

Olive oil

Salt and pepper

To cook

Preheat your oven to 180°C/gas mark 4.

Place the potatoes on a baking tray, then drizzle with olive oil. Scatter over a pinch of salt, then roast for about 35 minutes until cooked through.

Once cooked, transfer the potatoes to a saucepan over a medium heat. Add the butter, garlic, asparagus and peas, then season. Once it starts to sizzle, cook for about 3 minutes, then serve topped with chopped parsley and grated Parmesan.

SAUSAGE, KALE & BLACK BEAN STEW

By using tinned black beans as a clever cheat, this quick-cook stew has a rich depth of flavour normally associated with a much longer three- or four-hour cooking time. So, next time you're craving some comfort food, give this recipe a go.

To make one portion

2 sausages, cut into bite-sized chunks

1 garlic clove, sliced

200g black beans (from a 400g tin)

Handful of kale, chopped

Olive oil

Salt and pepper

To cook

Pan-fry the sausages in a splash of olive oil over a medium heat for about 15 minutes, until they are nicely coloured and cooked through, then add the garlic and fry for a further minute. Add the black beans (including half the liquid from the tin), season with salt and pepper and simmer for a few minutes before adding the kale (add a splash more water if you need to).

Simmer for a minute or so until the kale is nicely wilted, then serve with a generous pinch of cracked black pepper to garnish.

POTATO & BROCCOLI FRITTATA

This is a bit like a Spanish omelette, but with a couple of shortcuts and a few extra ingredients. Frittatas are a great way to use up leftovers – you can swap the ingredients around depending on what you have in the fridge.

To make one portion

A few baby potatoes, halved

A few slices of onion

A few pieces of long-stem broccoli

3 eggs, beaten

Small handful of crumbled feta cheese

Olive oil

Salt and pepper

To cook

Preheat your oven to 180°C/gas mark 4.

Place the potatoes in a baking tray and drizzle with olive oil. Sprinkle over some salt, then place in the oven. After 10 minutes, add the onions to the tray and return to the oven. After another 10 minutes, add the broccoli and roast for 10 minutes more. Remove from the oven and set aside.

Add a splash of oil to a small non-stick frying pan over a medium heat. Add the eggs and season, then add the roasted potatoes, onions and broccoli.

Cook for a few minutes, adding plenty of cracked black pepper. Cover the pan with a lid, baking tray or plate and cook for a few more minutes until the eggs are cooked through. Crumble over some feta cheese and serve.

GOLDEN SYRUP BROCCOLI NOODLES

Eating on a budget can be fun if you cook stuff that you like, and this is a great example of a dish that makes me feel really happy every time I cook it.

To make one portion

A few stalks of broccoli

Sesame oil

1 garlic clove, crushed

Pinch of dried chilli flakes

1 tbsp golden syrup

1 tbsp soy sauce

¼ lime

Salt and pepper

To cook

Bring a pan of salted water to the boil and cook the noodles according to the packet instructions.

Meanwhile, pan-fry the broccoli in a splash of sesame oil for a couple of minutes, then add the crushed garlic and chilli flakes. Fry for a further minute or two, then add the golden syrup, soy sauce, 1 tablespoon of sesame oil, a squeeze of lime juice, some cracked black pepper, and a tablespoon of the cooking water from the noodles. Simmer for a couple of minutes then drain the noodles, add them to the pan, stir and serve. Sheet of dried wholewheat noodles.

HONEY & MUSTARD CHICKPEAS WITH SWEET POTATO MASH

It's nice to balance the sweetness of honey with the bite of mustard to create a classic flavour combination. Slightly syrupy and delicious chickpeas all mopped up with a sweet potato mash.

To make one portion

- 1 large sweet potato
- 2 spring onions, roughly chopped
- 1 carrot, sliced
- 200g chickpeas (from a 400g tin), drained
- 2 tsp wholegrain mustard
- 1 tsp honey
- 100ml single cream
- Olive oil
- Salt and pepper

To cook

Preheat the oven to 180°C/gas mark 4 and roast the sweet potato for 40 minutes. Alternatively, pierce it several times with a fork and cook in the microwave on high for 6 minutes.

Meanwhile, pan-fry the spring onions and carrot in a splash of olive oil over a medium heat for a few minutes, then add the chickpeas, mustard, honey and cream. Stir and simmer for a few minutes until it thickens a little. Season to taste.

Using a tablespoon, scoop out the flesh of the sweet potato and mash it with a fork. Serve the mash with the honey and mustard chickpeas.

> **Tip** Save the sweet potato skin and use it for loaded potato skins or stuff it like a taco for another meal.

DICED & ROASTED VEG LASAGNE

How do you make veg even tastier? You chop it up and roast it! By caramelising the sugars on the outside, you can make this lasagne even richer in flavour. I know it's not a traditional recipe, but I like mixing things up. You'll also notice it's only got one layer: that's so you don't have to spoon half of the veg out of the dish, just to spoon it back in again.

To make one portion

½ onion, roughly chopped

½ carrot, roughly chopped

½ courgette, roughly chopped

½ yellow pepper, roughly chopped

Pinch of dried oregano

200g chopped tomatoes (from a 400g tin)

1 garlic clove, grated

1 fresh lasagne sheet (or precook a dry sheet in boiling water for 5 minutes)

½ ball of mozzarella, thinly sliced

Sprinkling of grated Parmesan cheese

Olive oil

Salt and pepper

To cook

Preheat the oven to 180°C/gas mark 4.

Spread the veg out on a baking tray. Season with salt, pepper and a pinch of oregano, then drizzle with a generous amount of olive oil. Roast for about 30 minutes, giving it a stir halfway through.

Transfer the roasted veg to a suitably sized ovenproof dish. Add the chopped tomatoes and grated garlic, then stir and return to the oven for another 10 minutes.

Season to taste, then top with the lasagne sheet, some slices of mozzarella and a sprinkling of grated Parmesan. Cook for another 20 minutes until the cheese is golden brown, then serve.

LASAGNE SOUP

I thought it would be quite cool to use lasagne sheets in a soup –
a sort of lasagne crossed with a minestrone soup – and it worked!

To make one portion

½ onion, sliced

200g cannellini beans (from a
    400g tin), drained

200g chopped tomatoes (from
    a 400g tin)

Pinch of dried oregano

½ vegetable stock cube

2 dried lasagne sheets

Handful of kale

Salt and pepper

To cook

Pan-fry the onion in a splash of olive oil over a medium heat for
about 3 minutes. Once softened, add the beans, chopped tomatoes and oregano, crumble in the stock cube, and season with salt
and pepper.

Snap the lasagne sheets into big chunks and throw them into the
pan, adding a splash of water if they are not totally submerged.
Add the kale too, and simmer for about 10 minutes until the pasta
is cooked. Sprinkle with more black pepper, drizzle with a generous
glug of olive oil, and serve.

THE WHOLE SQUASH PASTA

This recipe uses the entire squash, even the skin and the seeds! They add a fantastic contrasting texture and are totally free – they come already included in the price of the squash, LOL.

To make 4 portions

1 butternut squash

450g pasta

A few sage leaves

Olive oil

Salt and pepper

To cook

Preheat your oven to 180°C/gas mark 4.

Peel your squash and chop it into 2cm cubes, keeping the seeds and peel to one side. Place the squash cubes on a baking tray and drizzle with olive oil. Season with plenty of salt and pepper, then roast for about 35 minutes.

Meanwhile, place the skins and seeds on a separate tray, spreading them out nicely. Drizzle with olive oil and season with salt and pepper, then put them in the oven for the final 15 minutes of the squash roasting time.

Meanwhile, cook the pasta in a pan of salted boiling water according to the packet instructions. Once cooked, drain and save a mugful of the pasta water.

Place the roasted butternut squash cubes in a blender, along with a big splash of the pasta cooking water and a generous glug of olive oil. Blend until smooth. Season to taste, then mix with the pasta. Serve topped with the sage leaves, crunchy squash seeds and crispy roasted squash skin.

DATE-NIGHT DINNERS

FILO-BAKED CAMEMBERT

This dish makes a perfect starter. Here I've wrapped a whole Camembert in pastry, so it'll stay together in the oven (which would be your main challenge with any other cheese). It works well with either jam or onion chutney.

To make one portion

5 sheets of filo pastry

1 tbsp jam or onion chutney

1 large Camembert cheese

1 tsp honey

Handful of crushed nuts (any type)

Wedge of red cabbage, shredded

1 green apple, cut into matchsticks

1 carrot, cut into matchsticks

Squirt of mayonnaise

1 tsp Dijon mustard

Salt and pepper

To cook

Preheat your oven to 160°C/gas mark 3 and line a baking tray with greaseproof paper.

Lay the filo sheets out on the lined baking tray, layered one on top of the other. Dollop the jam or chutney into the middle, spread it out a bit and then position your Camembert on top. Wrap the cheese in the filo, then turn the parcel over to show the neater side. Brush with honey and sprinkle with half the nuts. Bake in the oven for about 20 minutes until golden brown and melted in the middle.

Meanwhile, make the slaw by mixing the cabbage, apple and carrot with the mayo, mustard and remaining crushed nuts. Season, then serve with the filo-baked Camembert.

BURRATA POMODORO

Burrata is expensive, so if you can't find it for a decent price, this recipe works equally well with normal mozzarella. Just half a ball of this mild and creamy cheese will elevate an extremely simple tomato pasta into something far more extravagant and impressive (when really all you've done is put some cheese on it).

To make one portion

125g spaghetti

A few cherry tomatoes, halved (optional)

1 garlic clove, crushed

200g chopped tomatoes (from a 400g tin)

Pinch of dried oregano

½ ball burrata or mozzarella cheese

Fresh basil leaves, to serve (optional)

Olive oil

Salt and pepper

To cook

Cook the spaghetti in a pan of salted boiling water according to the packet instructions. Once cooked, drain and save a little of the pasta water.

Pan-fry the cherry tomatoes in a generous glug of olive oil over a medium–high heat for a few minutes, then add the garlic and continue to fry for a few more minutes. Next add the chopped tomatoes, then season with salt, pepper and oregano and cook for about 5 minutes more.

Mix the cooked spaghetti into the sauce, along with a drizzle of olive oil and a splash of pasta water. Transfer to a bowl and serve topped with burrata and some cracked black pepper, plus a couple of fresh basil leaves (if using).

HALLOUMI & COURGETTE KEBABS WITH A LEMON DRESSING

Kebabs are a fun and easy classic: just chop up the ingredients and stick them on a skewer. The clever part here is using ribbons of courgette so they cook quicker. I've also brushed these kebabs with a lemon and thyme marinade to infuse those flavours into the halloumi as it cooks.

To make one portion

A few cubes of halloumi

A few ribbons of courgette (see Tip)

juice of ¼ lemon

A few thyme sprigs

Salad (whatever you have)

Olive oil

To cook

Light a barbecue or preheat a griddle or frying pan over a medium heat.

Thread the halloumi cubes and courgette ribbons on to a skewer.

To make the marinade, mix together the lemon juice and a big glug of olive oil in a small bowl.

Place the skewer on the barbecue, griddle pan or frying pan and lightly brush on the marinade using the thyme sprig as a brush. Turn the skewer every couple of minutes until cooked on all sides. Enjoy with a salad, and add the thyme sprig brush to the serving dish as a garnish.

> Tip You can cut the courgette ribbons carefully with a knife, or simply use a potato peeler.

GENERAL TSO'S TOFU

This is a hugely popular dish in America, and no doubt it'll catch on soon in the UK. It's usually made with chicken, but here I have adapted it slightly to create a delicious and more sustainable tofu version.

To make one portion

Handful of cubed tofu

1 tbsp plain flour

1 garlic clove, sliced

2 spring onions, finely sliced

2 tbsp tomato ketchup

Splash of soy sauce

Pinch of dried chilli flakes

Pinch of sesame seeds

Sesame oil

Salt and pepper

To cook

Dust the tofu in the flour and a pinch of salt and pepper, then pan-fry in a splash of sesame oil over a medium–high heat for about 4 minutes on each side until golden brown. Add the garlic and spring onions and continue to cook. After a couple of minutes, when the garlic starts to brown, add the ketchup, soy sauce and chilli flakes, along with another splash of sesame oil. This will create the sauce. Simmer down for about 1 minute until sticky, then serve, garnished with sesame seeds.

AUBERGINE PARM BURGER

You probably already know that aubergine parmigiana is amazing, especially when it's topped with crispy breadcrumbs. I was trying to come up with a way of completely covering the aubergine with breadcrumbs (without it going soggy) – and the aubergine parm burger was born.

To make one portion

1 tbsp plain flour

1 egg, beaten

Handful of breadcrumbs

2 x 1.5cm slices of aubergine

200g chopped tomatoes (from a 400g tin)

Pinch of dried oregano

2 thin slices of mozzarella cheese

1 bread roll

Handful of rocket, to garnish

Olive oil

Salt and pepper

To cook

Put the flour in one bowl, the beaten egg in another, and the breadcrumbs in a third. Season the flour and breadcrumbs with salt and pepper. Grab your aubergine slices and dust in the seasoned flour, then dip in the beaten egg and finally in the seasoned breadcrumbs. Shallow-fry in a generous glug of oil over a low–medium heat for about 5 minutes on each side, or until golden brown and cooked through. Place some mozzarella on each aubergine slice. Preheat the grill to medium, then transfer the cheesy aubergine slices to the grill for a minute or so until the mozzarella melts.

In the same pan you used for the aubergine, mix together the chopped tomatoes and oregano and season with salt and pepper. Simmer over a medium heat for about 5 minutes until thick.

Assemble the layers of aubergine, mozzarella and tomato sauce in the bread roll to create a burger. Top with a little rocket then serve.

ULTIMATE £1 ROAST

You will have to work hard to turn these inexpensive ingredients into the ultimate roast.

To make one portion

3 tbsp dry stuffing mix

approx. 20ml water

1 chicken leg, bone in and skin on

1 large potato, peeled and cut into large chunks

A few Savoy cabbage leaves, cut into thin strips

1 tsp gravy granules

Olive oil

Salt and pepper

To cook

First, combine the stuffing mix with the water. Squash everything together using your fingers, then roll the stuffing into a cylindrical shape. Next, debone the chicken leg, keeping the skin on, and season the inside well. Lay the chicken leg skin-side down on a sheet of tin foil and place the stuffing in the middle. Wrap it tightly into a neat cylinder and twist each end of the foil to make it extra tight. Poach in boiling water for 25 minutes, then cool under cold running water and refrigerate for a minimum of 30 minutes (you can do this the night before).

When you are ready to cook your ultimate £1 roast, preheat the oven to 190°C/gas mark 5.

Rinse the potato chunks under cold running water, place in a pan of cold salted water and bring to the boil. Cook for roughly 10 minutes until they soften slightly (so you can pierce them with a fork but they do not break). Drain, then return them to the saucepan and drench them in a few very generous glugs of olive oil. Tip into a baking tray and roast for about 35 minutes, turning a couple of times, until golden and crispy.

While the potato cooks, peel the foil off the chicken and pan-fry it gently in a splash of olive oil over a low–medium heat for about 20 minutes. Keep turning the chicken with tongs to evenly brown the skin (make sure the chicken is hot throughout).

Just before serving, season and pan-fry the cabbage over a high heat for a couple of minutes in a splash of olive oil.

Mix the gravy granules with boiling water (according to the packet instructions) and enjoy your ultimate £1 roast.

PATCHWORK ROAST CHICKEN PIE

What do you do with all those leftover scraps of puff pastry? Simple, chuck them on top of this patchwork pie, which also features leftover roast potatoes, veg and shredded roast chicken – so it's basically a leftovers pie! If you're missing any of the ingredients listed here, you can leave them out or swap them for something else. I love this pie because the patchwork lid gives the filling a chance to bubble through, creating those gorgeous caramelised bits that you usually only get at the edges.

To make one portion

- 2 tsp plain flour
- 200ml milk
- Handful of cooked chicken (such as roast chicken), shredded
- Handful of leftover cooked veg (such as peas and carrots)
- Handful of leftover cooked potatoes
- 1 tsp mustard (any)
- Handful of grated Cheddar cheese
- Leftover strips of puff pastry
- 1 egg, beaten (optional)
- Olive oil
- Salt and pepper

To cook

Preheat your oven to 180°C/gas mark 4.

Add a glug of olive oil to a saucepan, then add the flour and cook over a medium heat for 1 minute. Begin to add the milk, a little at a time, stirring continuously until a sauce forms.

Remove from the heat and throw in the chicken, veg, potatoes, mustard and cheese. If the sauce is too thick, just add a splash more milk. Season to taste, then transfer the mixture to a suitably sized ovenproof dish. Top with the pieces of puff pastry, then brush with beaten egg (if you want an extra-luxurious finish). Bake in the oven for about 30 minutes until golden brown.

VEGAN MUSHROOM WELLINGTON

This is a vegan dream come true, perfect for special occasions.

··

4 onions, diced

1kg mushrooms, sliced

4 garlic cloves, sliced

A few sprigs of fresh thyme, leaves picked and stalks discarded (or 1 tsp dried thyme)

1 sheet of frozen vegan puff pastry, defrosted

Olive oil

Salt and pepper

To cook ···

Start by pan-frying the onions in a glug of olive oil over a low heat with a big pinch of salt for about 15 minutes until sticky and caramelised. Remove from the pan and put to one side. Pan-fry the mushrooms in a splash of olive oil over a medium heat for about 10 minutes, adding the garlic and thyme halfway through and seasoning to taste. Once the mushrooms are cooked, return the onions to the pan, mix it all together, then remove from the heat and allow to cool.

Preheat your oven to 180°C/gas mark 4 and line a baking tray with greaseproof paper.

Lay your puff pastry sheet on the lined baking tray, then spoon the filling in a line down the middle. Fold one side of the pastry over the other and seal the edges by pushing down gently with your fingers. Lightly score the top with a knife to create a criss-cross pattern, then brush with a little oil.

Bake in the oven for about 25 minutes, or until golden brown and flaky.

SPIRAL VEGETABLE TART

Looking at this dish, you might think you'd need fancy knife skills to pull it off, but the whole thing is a huge cheat! It's all done with a vegetable peeler. So, if you're looking for something impressive, then this is the dish for you. It involves very few ingredients, is easy to prep and has maximum visual impact.

To make one portion

½ red onion

1 courgette

1 carrot

1 potato

1 tsp dried oregano

1 egg

Olive oil

Salt and pepper

To cook

Preheat your oven to 190°C/gas mark 5.

Cut the red onion into very thin slices and then, using a vegetable peeler, cut the courgette, carrot and potato into thin strips. Lightly drizzle all the slices with olive oil, and season with some of the oregano and some salt and pepper.

Grab a few slices of each vegetable (don't forget the onion) and roll them into a small spiral on the worktop. Keep placing more strips of vegetables and slices of onion around the outside and build the spiral until it is roughly the size of your dish.

Crack the egg into the dish and whisk it with a fork, season with a pinch of oregano, salt and pepper, then place the spiral into the dish. Push the spiral down so the egg fills the small gaps in the spiral, then bake in the oven for about 30 minutes until the vegetables are cooked.

SAUTÉED BUTTER LEEKS WITH WILD RICE

Lately, I've really been enjoying the novelty of wild rice. Don't get me wrong, normal rice is perfectly fine: I just need an extra bit of excitement in my rice life to make me feel alive. Here, I've paired it with delicious buttery leeks.

To make one portion

½ mug of wild rice

½ leek, chopped into 1.5cm rounds

1 shallot, quartered

1 tsp Dijon mustard

1 tbsp butter

1 tbsp water

Salt and pepper

Olive oil

To cook

Cook the wild rice in a pan of water according to the packet instructions, until all the water is absorbed and the rice is cooked through.

Meanwhile, season the leek slices, then add them to a frying pan with the shallots and a glug of olive oil. Cook over a medium heat for 7 minutes, or until slightly coloured, then turn them over and cook for another 7 minutes, so they get coloured on both sides. Remove from the pan and set aside.

To make the sauce, keep the pan on the hob and increase the heat to high. Add the Dijon mustard, butter, water, and 1 tablespoon olive oil. Stir for a couple of minutes, then drizzle the sauce over the leeks and rice and serve.

> **Swap** If you prefer, you can swap the wild rice for regular rice.

ROASTED PANZANELLA

Roasting the ingredients of a traditional panzanella salad transforms it into a delicious main course meal with a much more intense flavour.

Handful of cherry tomatoes	Small handful of rocket
½ red onion, quartered	Drizzle of balsamic glaze
2 pinches of dried oregano	Olive oil
5 slices of ciabatta	Salt and pepper

To cook ....

Preheat your oven to 190°C/gas mark 5.

Put the cherry tomatoes and onion quarters in a roasting tray and drizzle with olive oil. Add a pinch of the oregano and a pinch each of salt and pepper, then roast in the oven for about 15 minutes.

Meanwhile, drizzle the ciabatta slices with olive oil and sprinkle over the remaining oregano. Toast on a hot griddle pan over a medium heat on both sides until nicely charred (you could pan-fry or oven-bake the ciabatta if you prefer).

Assemble the panzanella by placing the roasted vegetables on the toasted ciabatta slices, along with the rocket, and drizzle with olive oil and balsamic glaze.

PULLED BBQ MUSHROOMS

Shredded sticky BBQ mushrooms on a toasted bun with sweet potato fries and slaw . . . This is a hungerbusting plate of pub grub.

To make one portion

1 sweet potato, cut into chips

1 portobello mushroom

1 red onion, sliced

Big squeeze of tomato ketchup

1 tsp smoked paprika

1 tsp muscovado sugar

Small wedge of red cabbage, shredded

½ carrot, cut into matchsticks

1 tbsp mayonnaise

Bread roll, sliced and toasted

Olive oil

Salt and pepper

To cook

Preheat your oven to 190°C/gas mark 5.

Place the sweet potato chips on a lined baking tray, drizzle with olive oil and season with salt and pepper, then cook in the oven for about 30 minutes, turning occasionally.

Meanwhile, tear the mushroom into pieces with your hands and pan-fry with half the sliced onion in a splash of olive oil over a medium heat for about 10 minutes until the onions start to caramelise. Add a big squeeze of ketchup, the paprika and the sugar, then simmer for a few minutes until the sauce goes a dark brown colour.

To make the slaw, mix the shredded cabbage with the carrot and the remaining sliced red onion, then add a tablespoon of mayo and a pinch of pepper.

Serve the pulled BBQ mushrooms on a toasted bun with the slaw and sweet potato chips.

MEXICAN STUFFED PEPPERS

The sweetness of oven-roasted yellow pepper is perfect for this spicy Mexican-style couscous filling.

To make one portion ··

- 1 yellow pepper, halved lengthways and deseeded
- Handful of tinned red kidney beans
- 1 tsp ground cumin
- Pinch of dried chilli flakes
- 1 spring onion, roughly chopped
- 2 egg-cups of couscous
- 2 egg-cups of water
- Olive oil
- Salt and pepper

To cook ···

Preheat your oven to 190°C/gas mark 5.

Put the pepper halves cut-side up in a roasting tray. Drizzle them with olive oil and season with a pinch of salt, then roast in the oven for about 15 minutes until softened.

Meanwhile, pan-fry the kidney beans in a splash of olive oil over a medium heat, with the cumin and a pinch each of salt and pepper, for a few minutes until they start to pop. Add the chilli flakes and spring onion and cook for a couple more minutes, then remove from the heat and add the couscous, stirring to coat it in the cumin-infused oil. Add the water, mix together and leave for a few minutes for the couscous to plump up. Taste and season again, if required, then stuff the roasted pepper halves with the filling and serve.

YAKI SOBA

This is my £1 version of the famous Wagamama Yaki Soba noodles. The distinctive flavour comes from using leeks instead of onion and adding a pinch of curry powder. And it totally works!

To make one portion

¼ leek, sliced

Splash of sesame oil

Pinch of curry powder

¼ green pepper, sliced

A few mushrooms, sliced

Small handful of bean sprouts

100g udon noodles

1 egg

Pinch of sesame seeds

A few slices of carrot, cut into matchsticks

Salt and pepper

To cook

Pan-fry the leeks in a splash of sesame oil and a pinch of curry powder over a high heat. After a couple of minutes, once the leeks have softened, add the peppers, mushrooms and bean sprouts and continue to pan-fry for a few more minutes.

Cook the noodles as per the instructions on the packet then drain and add to the pan.

Move everything to the side of the pan and crack an egg into the empty side. Once the egg is about 80 per cent cooked, scramble with a wooden spoon and mix everything together. Season to taste and serve with a sprinkle of sesame seeds and some chopped carrot.

GREEN LENTILS & CURRIED AUBERGINE

By oven-roasting veg with oil and curry powder, you get extra charring, and these chewy, slightly burned edges bring so much depth and flavour to the dish. For this to work, though, you need space. So don't let the veg overlap: that's the trick!

To make one portion

½ aubergine, sliced into long wedges

1 onion, half cut into wedges, half diced

2 tsp curry powder

1 carrot, diced

1 garlic clove, sliced

200g green lentils (from a 400g tin), plus half the liquid from the tin

Splash of single cream, plus extra to serve

Olive oil

Salt and pepper

To cook

Preheat your oven to 180°C/gas mark 4.

Put the aubergine and onion wedges in an ovenproof dish, making sure they don't overlap. Drizzle with a splash of olive oil, then sprinkle over 1 teaspoon of the curry powder and season with salt and pepper. Toss to coat, then roast for about 25 minutes until nicely coloured.

Meanwhile, pan-fry the diced onion and carrot in a splash of oil over a medium heat for about 3–4 minutes. Add the garlic and cook for another 3 minutes until it starts to colour, then add the green lentils, along with the reserved liquid from the tin. Stir in the remaining teaspoon of curry powder and a splash of cream, and season.

Transfer the lentils to a shallow bowl, and top with a pile of the charred aubergine and onion. Garnish with another splash of cream, and serve.

CHORIZO & ROASTED RED PEPPER ORECCHIETTE

Don't worry if you can't be bothered to blend the red peppers: just chop them small and it'll be fine, trust me. The important thing is to make sure you put the oil in: that's the key to this recipe.

To make one portion

Handful of dried orecchiette pasta

A few slices of roasted red pepper from a jar, plus a big splash of the oil

Handful of cooking chorizo, sliced

Salt and pepper

To cook

Cook the orecchiette in a pan of boiling salted water according to the packet instructions. Once cooked, drain and save a little of the pasta water.

Pop the roasted red pepper slices in a blender, along with a big splash of oil from the jar, and blend until smooth.

Meanwhile, pan-fry the chorizo for a few minutes over a medium heat until it starts to char and its paprika-infused oils are released. Then add the blended red peppers, the orecchiette and a splash of the reserved pasta water. Stir to combine and cook for a couple more minutes, then season and serve.

AUBERGINE MILANESE

Here's my meat-free twist on a classic Italian dish. I really love the contrasting texture of the crispy seasoned breadcrumbs and the buttery soft aubergine.

To make one portion

1 tbsp plain flour

1 egg

Handful of breadcrumbs (grated stale bread)

1cm-thick slice of aubergine

100g spaghetti

¼ onion, diced

1 garlic clove, sliced

200g chopped tomatoes (from a 400g tin)

Olive oil

Salt and pepper

To cook

Bring a saucepan of salted water to the boil. Grab three shallow bowls. Put the flour in one, crack the egg into another and beat it, and put the breadcrumbs in the third. Season the breadcrumbs with salt and pepper. Coat the aubergine slice in flour, then the egg, then the breadcrumbs.

Pan-fry the aubergine in a splash of olive oil over a medium heat for about 7 minutes on each side until golden brown and cooked through.

While the aubergine is in the pan, add the spaghetti to the boiling water and cook until al dente.

In a separate pan, fry the onion and garlic in a splash of olive oil over a medium heat for a few minutes. Once the onions are cooked and just as the garlic starts to brown, add the chopped tomatoes, season with salt and pepper and simmer for about 10 minutes until the tomatoes have broken down to make a nice sauce. Using tongs, transfer the cooked pasta from the saucepan to the frying pan with the pasta sauce and stir. Serve with the breaded, fried aubergine.

GARLIC PORTOBELLO PAPPARDELLE

Pasta sauces don't get much simpler than olive oil and garlic, and it's an all-time classic combination that goes so well with mushrooms. The trick with this dish is to first cook the mushrooms over a high heat to intensify the depth of flavour and extract all the water before adding the garlic (otherwise the garlic will burn). Using lasagne sheets, you can cut your own extra-wide pasta strips to create this elegant but simple Garlic Portobello Pappardelle.

To make one portion

1 portobello mushroom, sliced

3 dried lasagne sheets

2 garlic cloves, sliced

Pinch of dried (or chopped fresh) parsley

Grating of Parmesan

Olive oil

Salt and pepper

To cook

Bring a pan of salted water to the boil. Meanwhile, season and pan-fry the sliced mushroom in a big glug of olive oil over a medium-high heat for 8–10 minutes until dark brown in colour.

Cook the lasagne sheets in the boiling water until al dente, then drain and cut them into wide strips.

Add more olive oil to the mushroom, add the garlic and fry until the garlic just starts to colour. Now, add the pasta and fry for a further 30 seconds.

Remove from the heat and garnish with the parsley and a generous grating of Parmesan.

PEA CANNELLONI

Frozen peas are such a versatile ingredient, and a great way of eating economically. With zero waste, they're ready at a moment's notice, straight from the freezer. But, instead of using them as a side dish, why not make them the star of the show with my take on an Italian classic – a fresh and vibrant Pea Cannelloni with a tangy feta cheese topping.

To make one portion

2 big handfuls of frozen peas

3 dried lasagne sheets

Small handful of crumbled feta cheese

Olive oil

Salt and pepper

To cook

Preheat your oven to 190°C/gas mark 5 and bring a pan of salted water to the boil.

Add the peas and the lasagne sheets to the boiling water and bring back to the boil. As soon as the water starts to boil (and the lasagne sheets are floppy), drain the peas, remove the part-cooked lasagne sheets and set them aside.

Put the peas in a bowl, pop them all with the back of a tablespoon to break their skins, then add a generous glug of olive oil and season with salt and pepper.

Place a few spoonfuls of peas on each lasagne sheet and roll them into tubes. Lay the filled tubes in a small ovenproof dish and scatter over the crumbled feta, adding a glug of olive oil and sprinkling over some cracked black pepper.

Cook in the oven for about 15 minutes, until the cheese starts to brown.

Remove from the oven then tuck in.

MOVIE NIGHT 'PICKY BITS'

ROOT VEG PEEL CRISPS

This is a great way of using up vegetable peelings, although if you prefer you can just grab a piece of veg and turn the whole thing into strips with a peeler. Here, I have used beetroot, parsnip and carrot.

To make one portion

Handful of root vegetable peelings (beetroot, parsnip, carrot)

Salt

Vegetable oil

To cook

Either heat a few inches of oil in a deep pan over a medium–high heat, or get out your deep-fat fryer and set it to a medium–heat high heat (180°C).Once the oil is hot, drop the veg peelings into the oil and cook for about 5–10 minutes, removing with a slotted spoon once they are nice and crisp. Place on a plate lined with kitchen towel to drain, and sprinkle with salt. Serve straight away.

> **Tip** To see if the oil is hot enough to begin frying, just drop a small piece of vegetable peel into the pan and see if it sizzles.

SPICY POTATO PEEL CHIPS

Next time you're peeling potatoes for a Sunday roast, just take a little more care with your peeling to get bigger pieces, and save them for this chip recipe (the peelings will keep in the fridge for 1 day).

To make one portion

Handful of potato peelings

Pinch of paprika

Olive oil

Salt

To cook

Preheat your oven to 180°C/gas mark 4.

Spread out the potato peelings on a baking tray. Sprinkle with the paprika and some salt, and drizzle with olive oil. Cook in the oven for about 25 minutes, or until golden brown, giving the tray a shake halfway through. Serve with your favourite dip.

VEG PEEL PAKORAS

Another idea for using up those vegetable peelings – have a go at making these tasty zero-waste pakoras. You can use any veg you like. Here, I used some carrot and potato peelings. I even chucked in some old coriander, but that is totally optional.

To make one portion

Handful of vegetable peelings (I used carrot and potato)

Handful of coriander (it doesn't matter if it's past its best)

3 tbsp chickpea flour

1 tsp curry powder

Splash of water

Vegetable oil

Salt and pepper

To cook

Either heat a few inches of oil in a deep frying pan over a medium heat, or get out your deep-fat fryer and set it to a medium heat (around 170°C).

In a bowl, mix together the vegetable peelings, coriander, flour, curry powder and a pinch of salt and pepper. Add a little water, a splash at a time, until you get a batter-like consistency. It should look as if you have coated the veg in a few tablespoons of yogurt.

Drop the mixture into the hot oil, adding 1 tablespoon at a time, and fry for about 3 minutes until golden brown.

Set aside on a plate lined with paper towels to drain while you cook the remaining pakoras, then serve.

> **Tip** To see if the oil is hot enough for you to begin frying, drop a small blob of batter into the pan. If it sizzles in the oil, you can start frying.

LEEK & POTATO SAMOSAS

What do you do with leftover potatoes? Simple: make some delicious samosas!

To make one portion

½ leek, roughly chopped

Handful of roasted or boiled potatoes

1 tsp curry powder

A few sheets of filo pastry

Beaten egg, for brushing (optional)

Olive oil

Salt and pepper

To cook

Preheat your oven to 180°C/gas mark 4.

Pan-fry the leek in a splash of olive oil over a medium heat for about 5 minutes, then add the potatoes and curry powder. Season and fry for another minute or so.

Cut the filo pastry into 6 rectangles measuring about 30cm x 10cm. Arrange them so that you have 3 rectangles, each 2 sheets thick. Place 1 tablespoon of filling into the middle of each rectangle and fold the pastry around it in a triangle shape. Brush the samosas with a little oil (or some beaten egg) and place on a baking tray. Bake for about 15 minutes until golden brown. These are great hot or cold.

BUTTERNUT BHAJIS

This recipe is my quirky take on the classic onion bhaji. Onion bhajis are very difficult to get right because of the water content in the onions and the need for a deep-fat fryer. So I switched it up to butternut squash, which works brilliantly. Now you can make restaurant-quality bhajis whenever you want using just a few simple ingredients and a frying pan.

To make one portion

¼ butternut squash, peeled and grated

2 tbsp plain flour

1 egg

2 tsp curry powder

2 tbsp yogurt

Pinch of dried mint

Olive oil

Salt and pepper

To cook

Mix the grated butternut squash in a bowl with the flour, egg and curry powder, then season with a pinch each of salt and pepper.

Heat a generous glug of olive oil in a frying pan over a medium heat. When it's hot use a spoon to dollop small amounts of the grated butternut squash mixture into the pan and shallow-fry the bhajis for about 4 minutes on each side. Drain on kitchen paper.

Combine the yogurt and dried mint in a bowl to make a cooling dip.

Serve the hot bhajis with the cooling dip.

BEETROOT LATKES

These latkes are deliciously crispy and the toasted cumin seeds give them an amazing flavour – perfect for dipping in cool mint yogurt.

To make one portion

1 raw beetroot

Pinch of cumin seeds

1 egg

2 tbsp gram flour (chickpea flour)

1 tbsp yogurt

Pinch of dried mint

Olive oil

Salt and pepper

To cook

Grate the beetroot into a bowl and add the cumin seeds, egg and gram flour, season then mix. Heat a pan and dollop in the mixture, then fry over a medium heat in a splash of oil for about 3 minutes on each side.

Mix the yogurt with the dried mint and then serve with the beetroot latkes.

BLINIS

Homemade blinis taste so much better than shop-bought, and they can be topped with anything. I like the peppery combination of horseradish and radish, with a bit of rocket and crème fraîche, but this could be a great opportunity to use up any leftovers in the fridge.

To make one portion

100g cold mashed potato	1 tsp creamed horseradish
1 medium egg	2 tbsp crème fraîche
50ml milk	A few rocket leaves
50g self-raising flour	Olive oil
A couple of radishes, sliced	Salt and pepper

To cook

Mix the mashed potato, egg, milk and self-raising flour in a bowl until it forms a thick batter, then season with a pinch each of salt and pepper.

Heat a glug of olive oil in a frying pan over a medium heat, then add dollops of the batter (the mixture should make about 5 blinis). Fry for a few minutes on each side until golden brown.

Next make the topping. Mix the sliced radishes with the horseradish and crème fraîche, and season with salt and pepper. Scatter a few rocket leaves onto the blinis and spoon over the topping.

OVEN DIM SUM

In my first book I created some amazing pan-fried gyoza with a pasta-style dough. But, to be honest, I very rarely have time to make them, so I decided I needed a new super-fast dim sum recipe that required a lot less effort.

To make one portion

3 sheets of filo pastry

Sesame oil

Small handful of cooked and peeled prawns

1 garlic clove, crushed

1 spring onion, sliced

Soy sauce

To cook

Preheat your oven to 190°C/gas mark 5.

Fold the filo sheets to make them 4-layers thick and about 10 x 10cm. Brush them with sesame oil and stuff them into three holes of a Yorkshire pudding tray. Add 2 prawns, a tiny bit of crushed garlic and some slices of spring onion to each one.

Bake in the oven for 20 minutes until the filo pastry is golden brown.

Serve with a soy sauce dip.

PEA FALAFEL

Frozen spinach is great for binding these falafels together without needing to use egg, and is the key to making these vegan bites so tasty.

To make one portion

Handful of frozen peas

3 blocks of frozen spinach (about 50g)

2 tbsp chickpea flour (gram flour)

1 tsp ground cumin

A few lettuce leaves

A few slices of red onion

A few slices of radish

Olive oil

Salt and pepper

To cook

Let the peas and spinach sit at room temperature to defrost (or use a microwave), then blitz in a food processor with the chickpea flour, cumin and a pinch each of salt and pepper.

Heat a splash of olive oil in a frying pan over a medium heat. Using a tablespoon, add dollops of the falafel mixture to the frying pan (the mixture should make about 6 falafels) and cook, turning them over after a couple of minutes, until nicely browned.

Serve the falafels on lettuce 'boats', with slices of onion and radish.

CABBAGE POTSTICKERS

It was too difficult to come up with an easy way to fold these into an elegant shape, so I settled for just folding them in half and scrunching the ends together.

To make one portion

A small wedge of Savoy cabbage, finely shredded

1 garlic clove, crushed

Splash of sesame oil

40g plain flour, plus extra for dusting

25g water

Splash of soy sauce, plus extra for dipping

Salt and pepper

To cook

Pan-fry the shredded cabbage and the crushed garlic in a splash of sesame oil over a medium heat for a few minutes. Season with salt and pepper, add a splash of soy sauce and continue to cook for a further couple of minutes until the cabbage is cooked and soft. Transfer the cabbage to a bowl to cool but keep the dirty pan for frying the potstickers later.

In a bowl mix together the flour and water along with a pinch of salt to create a dough. Knead on a floured worktop for a few minutes until smooth, then cut into 6 smaller balls. Dust each ball with flour and roll into a rough circle about 7cm in diameter. Trim to create a neat circle (either use a cookie cutter, knife or scissors) and then leave on the dusted worktop to dry out a little and firm up.

Turn the dough circles over, so the drier side is underneath. Add a teaspoon of cabbage filling to each, fold them in half and scrunch the edges together to create a seal. Then pan-fry in the same pan that you cooked the cabbage with the lid on for a few minutes. Once the bottoms are golden brown and the tops are cooked, remove from the pan and serve with a soy sauce dip.

ZUCCHINI FRITTI

Yes, these fries are made from courgette, but I promise they are just as good as chips – and way posher. They're delicious paired with the lemon mayo dip.

To make one portion ··

1 courgette, sliced into thin French fries

4 tbsp plain flour

Pinch of paprika

Squeeze of lemon juice

2 tbsp mayo

Oil, for deep-frying

Salt and pepper

To cook ··

Place the sliced courgette fries in a colander and sprinkle with salt, then leave to rest for 20 minutes to extract excess moisture. Quickly rinse them, then pat dry with a paper towel.

Meanwhile, heat your oil to about 180°C, either in a high-sided pan over a medium heat, or in a deep-fat fryer. To see if the oil is hot enough, drop in a small piece of courgette and see if it sizzles.

Put the flour in a bowl and season with a pinch of salt and a pinch of paprika. Dust the courgette pieces in the flour, then deep-fry in the hot oil for a few minutes until they start to colour. Work in very small batches to get the best crust, transferring the cooked fritti to a plate lined with paper towels while you cook the next batch.

Stir the lemon juice into the mayo in a small bowl, then serve alongside the zucchini fritti.

CAULI BUFFALO WINGS

Cauliflower florets are the perfect size and shape to make this meat-free alternative to buffalo wings. I use them here in the same way as chicken. You can use frozen cauliflower instead of fresh.

To make one portion

- 1 cauliflower (or frozen equivalent, defrosted)
- 2 tbsp flour
- 2 eggs
- Handful of breadcrumbs
- 1 tsp paprika

- 1 tbsp blue cheese
- 4 tbsp crème fraîche
- 1 spring onion, sliced
- Olive oil
- Salt and pepper

To cook

Preheat your oven to 190°C/gas mark 5 and line a baking tray with greaseproof paper.

Cut your cauliflower into florets. Grab three shallow bowls. Put the flour in one, crack the eggs into another and beat them, and put the breadcrumbs in the third. Season the flour with a pinch each of salt and pepper. Season the breadcrumbs and add the paprika and a tiny drizzle of olive oil. Dip the cauliflower florets in the flour, then the egg, then

the breadcrumbs and lay them out on the lined baking tray. Roast them in the oven for about 25 minutes or until golden brown.

Meanwhile, make a dipping sauce by mixing the blue cheese with the crème fraîche until smooth. Serve your wings with a garnish of spring onion and the dip.

SESAME PRAWN TOAST

It's fine to use cooked frozen prawns here: that's what I do, because that's what I have in my freezer. Also, it's difficult to save half an egg, so I usually double the quantities below to make 2 portions and save some for later.

To make one portion

Handful of defrosted cooked peeled prawns

1 spring onion, plus extra to serve

1 garlic clove

1 tsp soy sauce

½ egg, beaten

A few slices of any bread

Small handful of sesame seeds

½ carrot, cut into matchsticks

Small handful of lamb's lettuce (or any salad leaves)

Big dollop of sweet chilli sauce

Vegetable oil or sesame oil

Salt and pepper

To cook

Chuck the prawns, spring onion, garlic and soy sauce into a blender. Add the egg and blend to create a paste. Spread this paste over the bread.

Place the sesame seeds on a small plate, then dip each slice of the bread into the seeds.

Pan-fry the slices in a glug of oil over a medium heat for a minute or two on each side until golden brown. Serve with carrot matchsticks and salad leaves on the side, and a little bowl of sweet chilli sauce for dipping. Scatter over some sliced spring onion and enjoy.

BUBBLE & SQUEAK POTATOES

Bubble and squeak is a great example of a dish that was created with budget eating in mind. Here, I have added a modern twist by stuffing potato skins, using the same classic flavours.

To make one portion

3 medium or small potatoes

¼ Savoy cabbage, shredded

Olive oil

Salt and pepper

To cook

Preheat your oven to 190°C/gas mark 5.

Pierce the potatoes skins and cook them (skin on) in the microwave for 10 minutes or in the oven for about 35 minutes (the cooking time will depend on the size of the potatoes). Cut the cooked potatoes in half and scoop out the middles. Put the potato skins to one side.

Meanwhile, pan-fry the cabbage in a splash of olive oil over a medium heat with plenty of salt and pepper for about 4 minutes. Once the cabbage is cooked, mix in the scooped-out potato, season once more and add a big glug of olive oil. Spoon the potato filling back into the potato skins, place them on a baking tray and cook in the oven for 15–20 minutes. Remove from the oven and serve.

SPICY PATATAS BRAVAS

Instead of the usual tomato-based sauce, here I've switched it up to a roasted red pepper sauce with a spicy kick.

To make one portion

Handful of small potatoes, skin on

200g roasted red peppers (from a 400g jar), plus half the oil

Squirt of sriracha

Pinch of dried oregano

1 spring onion, roughly chopped

Olive oil

Salt and pepper

To cook

Cook the potatoes in a pan of salted boiling water for about 15 minutes until soft. Drain and let them steam for a bit to dry out.

Transfer the potatoes to a frying pan and squash each one slightly with the back of a fork to break the skins and expose the fluffy middle. Season and fry the potatoes in a generous glug of olive oil for about 20 minutes until crispy all over.

Meanwhile, to make the sauce, grab a blender and add the roasted red peppers, along with the oil from the jar, the sriracha, oregano and a pinch of salt. Blend and then pour into the pan with the potatoes. Simmer for a couple of minutes to warm the sauce, then add the chopped spring onion and some cracked black pepper, and serve.

PARTY PIZZAS

These quick and easy baked filo pizzas are fun finger food and great for parties.

To make one portion

6 square sheets of filo pastry (about 20 x 20cm)

Handful of cherry tomatoes, quartered

Handful of grated mature Cheddar cheese

6 slices of chorizo

Pepper

To cook

Preheat your oven to 190°C/gas mark 5.

Grab a muffin tin and fold each sheet of filo in half, then in half again, to make six 10cm squares.

Using your fingertips, press a filo square into six of the holes in the tin to create cup shapes. Throw in enough chopped cherry tomatoes to fill each cup about three-quarters full, season with pepper and top with some grated cheese and a slice of chorizo.

Cook in the oven for about 20 minutes, taking them out of the muffin tin after 10 minutes, placing them on a baking tray and putting them back in the oven for the final 10 minutes of baking. This guarantees the bases get nice and evenly toasted.

DETROIT PIZZA

I've taken out every superflous step to create this amazingly simple but really tasty pizza with a characteristic Detroit-style square shape and thick crust.

To make one portion

150g self-raising flour, plus extra for dusting

100ml cold water

4 tbsp passata

Pinch of dried oregano

Big handful of grated Cheddar cheese

6 pepperoni slices

Salt and pepper

To cook

Preheat your oven to 190°C/gas mark 5.

Using a spoon, mix the flour and water together in a bowl along with a big pinch of salt to form a dough. Dust the worktop with a little flour then knead the dough on the worktop for a minute or two until smooth. Roll it into a rectangle. Lay the dough onto a 15 x 23cm baking tray (increase the ingredient quantities if you are using a bigger tray) and push the dough into the edges and corners. Spread the passata over the top, leaving a border around the edge, and season with salt and pepper. Sprinkle over the oregano and cheese and top with the pepperoni slices, then bake in the oven for about 20 minutes until the base is cooked and the cheese is nicely melted.

SAUTÉED TINNED POTATO NACHOS

It's time consuming to make the perfect sautéed potatoes, as it involves multiple steps and multiple pans. So here is my shortcut using tinned potatoes.

To make 4 portions

2 x 300g tins of potatoes, drained

1 tsp ground cumin

Handful of cherry tomatoes

Squirt of sriracha

1 avocado, sliced

2 tbsp crème fraîche

2 spring onions, sliced

Handful of feta cheese, crumbled

Handful of fresh coriander, chopped

Olive oil

Salt and pepper

To cook

Thinly slice your potatoes, lightly dust with cumin and then pan-fry in batches in a generous splash of olive oil over a medium to high heat. Season and then set to one side on some kitchen paper.

Meanwhile, make your salsa by chopping your tomatoes, seasoning and mixing with a squirt of sriracha.

Place the potatoes in a serving dish and top with the salsa, sliced avocado, crème fraîche, spring onions, feta and coriander.

RADIATOR FOCACCIA

You're not going to believe that you can make such beautiful bread so easily. I've even taken out all the kneading steps so you won't get your worktop messy. This really is the simplest bread you'll ever attempt and your radiator does most of the hard work for you.

To make one portion

250g strong flour

200ml lukewarm water

7g sachet of dried yeast

A few cherry tomatoes (on the vine)

A few spring onions

1 tsp dried oregano

Olive oil

Salt and pepper

To cook

Grab a bowl and throw in the flour, water and yeast along with a big pinch of salt. Mix it all together using a spoon to create a wet dough. Transfer the dough to an oiled baking tray, wrap with cling film and place in a warm place, like next to a radiator, for 1 hour.

Preheat your oven to 190°C/gas mark 5.

After the dough has risen, unwrap the tray, drizzle over some olive oil and spread the dough out to fill the whole tray. Make lots of indentations in the dough using your fingertips then add the tomatoes and spring onions, pushing them into the dough. Sprinkle over some salt and pepper, along with the oregano and a splash more olive oil, then bake in the oven for 25 minutes until golden brown.

POTATO FOCACCIA

Cutting potatoes in a spiral increases the surface area when cooking, and makes them twice as crispy. But if you want a quicker method, just slice the potatoes instead, and scatter over some chopped rosemary.

To make one portion

100g strong flour

3.5g dried yeast

100ml warm water

4 small potatoes

4 rosemary sprigs

Olive oil

Salt and pepper

To cook

Grease a 20 x 10cm oven tray with oil. Put the flour, yeast and water in a bowl along with a pinch of salt, and mix to form a dough. Tip the dough into the greased oven tray, drizzle the dough with olive oil, cover with cling film and leave in a warm place for 1 hour.

Preheat your oven to 190°C/gas mark 5.

Grab a potato and skewer it from end to end with a chopstick. Cut into the potato in a spiral formation, from one end to the other (the chopstick will prevent you cutting all the way through the potato), then remove the chopstick and insert a sprig of rosemary in its place, stretching out the potato spiral along the sprig to open it up.

Repeat with the remaining potatoes and rosemary sprigs then drizzle them with olive oil and season with salt and pepper. Once the dough has risen, remove the cling film, squash the skewered, spiral potatoes into the dough and bake in the oven for about 30 minutes until golden brown.

CAULIFLOWER TACOS

By making your own tortillas, this dish comes in at well under £1.

¼ cauliflower

Pinch of cumin seeds

Squirt of sriracha

2 tbsp mayonnaise

40g plain flour

25ml cold water

Handful of thinly sliced red cabbage

½ red onion, thinly sliced

Small handful of chopped coriander

½ lime

Olive oil

Salt and pepper

To cook

Cut the cauliflower into florets, then pan-fry them in a splash of olive oil and a pinch each of salt and pepper over a medium heat for a few minutes, until the cauliflower starts to colour. Add the cumin seeds and fry for a few more minutes until the cauliflower is tender. Remove from the heat and set to one side. Combine the sriracha and mayo in a small bowl.

To make the tacos, put the flour and water in a bowl with a pinch of salt and mix to create a dough. Knead on a work surface until the dough is smooth, then separate it into three pieces and roll each piece into a ball. Roll each ball into a circle about 10cm in diameter. Heat a frying pan over a high heat. Toast the tacos in the hot pan one at a time for a few minutes on each side until lightly toasted.

To make the salad, mix the cabbage and onion in a bowl, add the coriander and squeeze over the juice from the half lime. Add a splash of olive oil and season, then let it rest for about 10 minutes to soften the onion in the lime juice. Assemble the tacos, placing a few florets on a bed of the salad, and top with the sriracha mayo.

SHREDDED CHICKEN TACOS

I love tacos with slow-cooked pork shoulder, but it takes hours and hours to really break down that meat. So save some electricity (and some time!) with my much quicker chicken version, ready in about 30 minutes.

To make one portion

2 chicken drumsticks, skin removed

½ onion, sliced

Pinch of ground cumin

Pinch of paprika

200g chopped tomatoes (from a 400g tin)

A few soft-shell tacos or tortillas

Crumbled feta, for sprinkling

A few slices of red onion

A few sprigs of coriander

Olive oil

Salt and pepper

To cook

Season the chicken, then pan-fry over a medium heat in a splash of olive oil. After about 7 minutes, add the onion and continue to fry for a further 5 minutes. Next add the cumin, paprika and chopped tomatoes. Cook for 15–20 minutes, until the chicken is cooked through. Remove the chicken from the pan and use two forks to shred the meat from the bone. Return the shredded meat to the pan and stir through the sauce.

Load up your tacos with the chicken and tomato mixture, and top with some crumbled feta, red onion and coriander.

> **Tip** You can use up the rest of the tinned tomatoes in one of my other recipes – try the Pasta Alla Norma on page 70.

INDEX